WADSWORTH PHILOSOPHERS SERIES

W9-BOK-021

ON

HOBBES

Marshall Missner
University of Wisconsin Oshkosh

Wadsworth
Thomson Learning.

Australia • Canada • Denmark • Japan • Mexico • New Zealand • Philippines
Puerto Rico • Singapore • Spain • United Kingdom • United States

Printed in the United States of America
1 2 3 4 5 6 7 03 02 01 00 99

For permission to use material from this text, contact us:
Web: www.thomsonrights.com
Fax: 1-800-730-2215
Phone: 1-800-730-2214

For more information, contact:
Wadsworth/Thomson Learning
10 Davis Drive
Belmont, CA 94002-3098
USA
www.wadsworth.com

ISBN: 0-534-57592-7

CONTENTS

ACKNOWLEDGMENTS

I would like to thank Ann Hoeft-Trabbold and Milton Goldinger for their patience and technical wizardry in helping me to learn the intricacies of a new word-processing program. Their generosity belies some of Hobbes' favorite claims about human nature.

1
Introduction

"Why can't we all just get along together?" That was the plaintive question Rodney King asked after Los Angeles exploded in riots in 1992 after an all-white jury acquitted some policemen who were videotaped viciously beating the African-American Mr. King.

It is an interesting question. Just why can't we all get along? Why are there all of the fights and beatings and death? Why do human beings continue to wage war and brutalize each other century after century? The benefits of peace seem so obvious and so desirable, and anyone can see that cooperation will make everyone better off. But yet it goes on--in every continent, in every country, in almost every neighborhood, and in many, many homes. The constant battle. Yet, we also have to admit that life is not a continual war. People do live in peace and they do cooperate in activities for mutual benefit, at least for a time. There is this strange cycle of fighting and cooperating--neither one being stable. Why is that?

The philosopher Thomas Hobbes devoted most of his career and his thought to investigating these disturbing problems. These were not just interesting academic questions for him, for he lived in England in the 17th Century during a civil war and he saw the viciousness that so quickly comes to the fore. He set himself the task of determining once and for all just why it is that human beings have so much trouble living with each other, and he also presented his understanding of why the war between people is not drearily continual, for at times peace does emerge.

Whether his diagnoses and analyses were accurate, it is clearly the case that these problems are still with us. Peace and cooperation are not everywhere and are fragile even where they do exist. Maybe by studying Hobbes' thought, we might get some clues about why this perennial situation endures, and perhaps we can get some ideas of what we could do to improve matters. On the other hand, it could be that Hobbes' views are all wrong. But even if wrong, Hobbes' ideas are thoughtful, imaginative, and the product of an extremely powerful and fertile mind, and whatever our final verdict is on their cogency, we can will probably learn something important, even if it is only that a very persuasively argued view is mistaken.

The main focus of this book about Hobbes' philosophy will be his views about war and peace--why people fight, and why they live together in peace. Hobbes thought about these questions for a number of decades, and he developed insightful and interesting answers to them. We will see the major outlines of his views, how they developed during the course of his life, and then assess whether he finally did crack this very hard nut.

But war and peace were not the only areas of concern for Hobbes, and even in his discussion of those crucial issues, he related them to other aspects of philosophy. In particular, Hobbes was fascinated by the developing science of his times, the 17th Century, and especially by the mechanical and materialistic views that were being presented by Galileo and others. Hobbes thought that materialism had implications for the topics of free will, religion and the nature of human beings. He followed these implications with rigor and perseverance, even when it was clear that he was treading on very dangerous orthodox grounds. We will also examine what Hobbes had to say about these other matters of interest, and see how they all were related to the questions of why people fight, and what makes them stop, put down their weapons and live in peace.

Hobbes the Writer

Hobbes thought that he had the key to producing peace in his time, but it would be of little value if he presented his views in such a way that it could not be understood, and so Hobbes made great efforts to make his writing lively and accessible. Hobbes was not writing in an academic atmosphere where he was just trying to convince other philosophers; rather, he was living in an unstable and divided country, that had suffered through a civil war and that could plunge into it again in a moment.

It was thus important for him to write in a way that would be clear, and yet engaging, a way that would persuade all of those who could read, and those who could just listen. Given these goals, Hobbes' resources as a writer were substantial to say the least, for he had rhetorical capacities probably unmatched in the history of English speaking philosophy. Hobbes' style was forceful and punchy, and he had a facility for creating short and memorable phrases. Hobbes was the author of what is probably the most famous phrase of philosophy written in English--that life in the state of nature is "solitary, poor, nasty, brutish and short." Among Hobbes' other well-known maxims were that men associate for "gain and glory" and that the two cardinal virtues of war are "force and fraud."

Hobbes also had the poetic ability to develop striking images that became part of the expression of his theories. Few others would have had the literary nerve to entitle their main work of political philosophy, *Leviathan*. This is an image Hobbes elaborated in his book--the state as a horrifying and fearful monster that will scare people into keeping their agreements.

Another quality that Hobbes used in his works is a gift for satire and irony. Consider this passage from the very beginning of *De Cive*, in which Hobbes was trying to deny that people associate with each other for the mere pleasure of sociability, but instead, always have some other purpose that they are trying to accomplish.

We do not therefore by nature seek society for its own sake, but that we may receive some honor or profit from it; these we desire primarily, that secondarily. How, by what advice, men do meet, will be best known by observing those things which they do when they are met. For if they meet for traffic, it is plain every man regards not his fellow, but his business; if to discharge some office, a certain market-friendship is begotten, which hath more of jealousy in it than true love, and whence factions sometimes may arise, but good will never; if for pleasure and recreation of mind, every man is wont to please himself most with those things which stir up laughter, whence he may, according to the nature of that which is ridiculous, by comparison of another man's defects and infirmities, pass the more current in his own opinion. And although this be sometimes innocent and without offence, yet it is manifest they are not so much delighted with the society, as their own vain glory. But for the most part, in these kind of meetings we wound the absent; their whole life, sayings, actions are examined, judged, condemned. Nay, it is very rare but some present receive a fling as soon as they part; so as his reason was not ill, who was wont always at parting to go out last. And these are indeed the true delights of society, unto which we are carried by nature, that is, by those passions which are incident to all creatures, until either by sad experience or good precepts it so fall out, which in many never happens, that the appetite of present matters be dulled with the memory of things past: without which the discourse of most quick and nimble men on this subject, is but cold and hungry.

This passage was not just included in *De Cive* for the amusing and sardonic picture it painted of gossiping and egotistical Englishmen, for Hobbes was using it in that work to establish a critical point for his entire view. Nevertheless, it is difficult not to laugh out loud when one reads it, or just smile in recognition as we remember the "flings" we may have thrown at the absent on occasion. While some might protest that this is too narrow a view of human interaction, there is nevertheless something to what Hobbes was saying and it was presented in such an energetic, striking way, that we are swept along and persuaded that Hobbes' point may indeed be true.

Even in the most technical portions of Hobbes' works, there are some little jewels of phrasing or imagery. Also, Hobbes did not confine his literary abilities to works of philosophy. He wrote an autobiography in verse, and at the end of his life, when the King prohibited him from publishing any more treatises in philosophy, he amused himself by writing a verse translation of Homer's *Iliad*.

General Summary of Hobbes' View

It will be useful to have an overview of the general kind of argument that Hobbes developed in his political philosophy. He wrote three different versions of his political philosophy, and in the later versions he tried to address the weak points of the earlier versions and thus construct a Leviathan of his own that could swallow any objections raised against it.

Hobbes began every one of his versions of his political philosophy by providing an account of the core universal features of human beings. In two of the three versions of his philosophy, this account is quite extensive and detailed, but in one of the versions, the above-mentioned *De Cive*, the account is very brief. Nevertheless, Hobbes thought that in order to understand why we fight, and also why we make peace, we must begin with an understanding of the fundamental characteristics of human beings. These characteristics incline us to not cooperate with each other, and so without some other intervening factor, we humans would be living in a constant state of war. But we are clever animals, and we can think of a way to get out of this terrible situation. We have the capacity to think of arrangements where we agree to inhibit those features that lead us to fight. But the agreement will only work if people stick to it, and also if we have the confidence that others will not betray us. What will provide that confidence? Only some overwhelming force that everyone knows will punish those that break the agreement. Our problem then is to figure out how to construct that force.

Many have seen Hobbes as having a very dark and gloomy view of human beings, one that is much too negative and that over-emphasizes our hostile traits and ignores our more sympathetic and altruistic impulses. While this criticism of Hobbes is exaggerated, it is still the case that Hobbes' view cannot be characterized as one of the most tender-hearted and optimistic accounts of human nature that have been given over the centuries. Hobbes was not concerned to provide a view of human nature that was uplifting and that would make people feel wonderful about themselves and others. After all, if people were really so nice, why is there the difficult and perennial problem of war and peace? In order to provide a solution to the problems we face, Hobbes thought it was necessary to look at ourselves honestly and realistically to discover what the sources are of our troubling difficulties.

In developing his solution, Hobbes tried to avoid using any moral notions of what would be the right way to live, or any theological views about what God demands of us. His main reason for avoiding morality and theology in his theory was that people have such varied views about what is moral and about what God has commanded us to do. In fact, these varied views were one of the main causes of the civil war that was creating havoc in England at this time. In order to present a theory that would be acceptable to all people, Hobbes attempted to avoid all reference to moral or theological premises. He would make no assumptions what God was like or what He said. He would also make no assumptions about what traits are virtuous and whether there is some one over-riding goal of human life. He would just consider human beings as they are, and on that basis provide answers to the questions of why there is so much conflict and how we can avoid it. If his answers were successful, then Hobbes hoped that no one would be able to object to them because of the ideas they had about morality or theology.

2
War

What Methods Can Be Used to Find the Answers?

Like his famous contemporary, Rene Descartes, and other philosophers of the 17th Century, Hobbes had a great interest in matters of method. In order to find answers to an important question, Hobbes believed it was first necessary to have a conception of what would be the proper method to use for the particular issue. Finding the appropriate method was considered to be the most important, as well as the most difficult, part of an enquiry, for once the right method was obtained, it could be used it to generate the correct answer.

But there is another aspect to be considered in this matter of method. Hobbes realized that people not only have a variety of moral and theological views, but they also use very different ways of finding answers to questions. The methods that seem appropriate to some would seem crude to others, and the rigorous and technical methods that some people would be inclined to use, would appear baffling and unnecessary to other people. People are very different in their sophistication and in their cultural and educational backgrounds, and this affects what methods they are willing to use. Hobbes knew that there is universal concern about the problems of war and peace, but even if he avoided moral and theological assumptions, he would not provide an answer to convince everyone, if he just used the kind of method that appeals to one group of people. To widen the range of those he would appeal to, he thought it was important to provide different kinds of arguments that would be suitable to different kinds of audiences. In general Hobbes developed two ways to support his view, one that will be called the intellectual way (Hobbes called it "science") and the other that will be named the way of ordinary experience (Hobbes called this method "prudence"). Of course, Hobbes was aware that intellectual types also have ordinary experience, at least once in a while. But often, those convinced by one of these methods are not impressed by the other. Hobbes thought that he could develop the same kind of theory, with the same conclusions and proposals with both methods, and by using both, he would increase the range of people that would be persuaded by his views.

One qualification has to be made to what has been said about Hobbes' two methods and his avoidance of theology. Anyone who looks at *Leviathan* (Hobbes' most developed and mature statement of his political views) will notice that the second half of the book concerns religion, and there are many points in the book where Hobbes quotes the Bible in support of his views. But this does not contradict the claim that Hobbes used just two methods in his political works to establish his conclusions. Hobbes lived in a time when the Bible was considered not to be just a religious book, as it was also thought to contain the most profound wisdom on all subjects. There is a good deal of doubt whether Hobbes believed this himself, but he realized that most of his contemporaries did hold this view. In order to convince them of his theories, Hobbes thought that it would be helpful to show that everything that he said was Biblically supported. Whether this was the case of the Devil quoting Scripture, as many of Hobbes' enemies said, will be discussed below. But even if one grants that Hobbes sincerely thought that his views were compatible with the Bible, he clearly did not use the Bible in developing his ideas, nor did he think it was necessary to use the Bible in order to prove that his ideas were true. The intellectual way and the way of ordinary experience were the methods he would use for those two purposes. The quotations from the Bible were just a way to make his views more palatable and acceptable.

Hobbes' Method of Science--The Intellectual Way

Geometry

One of the famous anecdotes about Hobbes' life was told by his contemporary, James Aubrey, in a book entitled *Brief Lives*. The story concerns Hobbes' discovery of geometry.

"He was 40 years old before he looked on Geometry; which happened accidentally. Being in a Gentleman's Library, Euclid's Elements lay open and 'twas the 47 El. libri I. He read the Proposition. By G___, said he (he would now and then swear an emphatical Oath by way of emphasis) this is impossible! So he reads the Demonstration of it, which referred him back to such a Proposition; which proposition he read. That referred him back to another, which he also read. Et sic deinceps [and so on] that at last he was demonstratively convinced of that truth. This made him in love with Geometry."

This charming little paragraph is interesting for a number of reasons. One is that it is quite shocking that Hobbes, who had been educated at Oxford, had never been exposed to Euclid's Geometry until he was a middle-aged man. But the most significant point is that Hobbes developed an appreciation for the method used in geometry. This is the axiomatic method that could well be the most powerful intellectual device available to us humans. What appealed to Hobbes about it was that it was a method of compelling proof. One could present a statement, and if someone thought that the statement was not true, one could show how it followed from some more basic statement, and if questions were raised about the more basic statement, one could be referred to an even more basic statement. The result of all of this is a structure, where each level is supported by lower levels, and once the lower levels are accepted, then everything follows in a logical and rigorous way that cannot be denied.

It is obvious that in this kind of structure the soundness of the upper levels depends on the solidity of the foundation. If somehow one can begin with incontrovertible foundation statements, and then build on them with careful reasoning, then like it or not, anyone capable of understanding will have to accept what is presented at the higher levels.

It was Hobbes' dream to develop a system of this kind that would have as its higher level, statements about the causes of war and the solutions for peace. His hope was that he could make an axiomatic system that would have the same power as Euclid's geometry. In geometry anyone capable of thinking and reasoning has to admit that Euclid's conclusions about triangles, squares and circles have to be true. Everything follows from the initial premises. Hobbes' goal in all the versions of his work on war and peace was to produce the same kind of logical system. A reader may disagree with some statement that Hobbes made about the causes of war and what is necessary to make peace. But if so, Hobbes thought he could use his system to take the reader by the scruff of the neck and say the following. "The statement you disagree with is based on some more basic one, and that one on an even more basic one, and so on until we reach the foundation that you cannot deny, and so like it or not, you must relinquish your disagreement with that particular statement."

But what is the foundation that no one can deny? What could Hobbes use to build this kind of powerful axiomatic system? In order to answer this question, it is necessary to give a brief account of Hobbes' views about our ideas, the language we use to refer to them, and the way we use language to reason.

Materialism

Hobbes had an interesting theory about how the world worked that was very much influenced by his contact with the leading intellectuals of his time, particularly the great scientist, Galileo in Italy. Galileo had adopted the view of materialism, a view that had been presented in antiquity by the Greek philosopher, Democritus and the Roman philosopher, Lucretius. Hobbes' version of materialism was based on the assumption that all existing things are pieces of matter, that move around in the void of space. These pieces of matter clang into each other, and the bigger ones push the smaller ones around according to certain mechanical laws of motion. At times some of the pieces of matter stick together to form the physical objects that we perceive. Our own bodies are also combinations of these little clumps of stuff, and so the laws of motion that govern the behavior of inanimate physical objects also apply to us. All of our behavior can be considered as a mechanical process consisting of the little corpuscles banging into and moving other corpuscles.

That is how our senses, and more particularly, how vision works. Particles from the external world strike our eyes, and set in motion a cascade of effects that lead to what Hobbes charmingly calls a "phantasm" and that would later be called an idea. A phantasm is just a collection of particles (Hobbes calls them "subtle particles") that occur inside one's body that are caused by events and objects that happen outside of the body and that in some way represent these objects and the events. Suppose that we are watching a baseball game. In Hobbes' materialistic account, particles from the players and the field strike our eyes and start a chain of causes in our brains, and somehow, there is an image of the game in our heads, made up of some special subtle bits of matter.

Hobbes considered this materialist view to be a basic axiom and thus, a foundation of his whole view of how people behave and what motivates them to act the way they do. But it would certainly be asking us to accept a great deal to have us just accept this view as being obvious and as not requiring any supporting argument. Hobbes realized this and he did present some reasons why materialism should be accepted that will be discussed in a later chapter. But in setting forth his views on war and peace, he just claimed that materialism as a basic fact about the world. Let us allow him this point in order to see where it leads.

Language

So here we are with a group of phantasms that are clanging around inside of us. We note, in a way that is not clear at all, that there is some similarity among a group of these phantasms and we provide a label to remind ourselves of this similarity. This is the origin of language, according to Hobbes. A word is just a label for a group of phantasms, and sentences are just combinations of words. Every sentence can be reduced or analyzed into the original motions of the senses. Thus, to take a most hackneyed philosophical example, consider the sentence, 'all men are mortal'. The basic elements of this sentence are the two labels, 'men' and 'mortal', and it is not a difficult exercise to break these terms down into their constituent parts. The labels stand for phantasms that form inside of us by being exposed to various objects that are relatively hairless, that have two legs, two arms, and a rather large, round head, that walk upright and utter all kinds of sounds. There is another group of phantasms that are caused by the sight of objects drooping, and then falling, and then finally not moving at all. Without our senses, we would not have any of these phantasms, but since we do have senses that are affected by external objects, we have a vast storehouse of phantasms that we can name and combine, and thus we produce language.

Reasoning

As combinations of phantasms lead to words, and combinations of words lead to sentences, combination of sentences lead to reasoning. To consider another hackneyed example, the sequence of statements, All men are mortal; Socrates is a man; and so Socrates is mortal, is a combination of statements that enables us to draw out a conclusion. According to Hobbes, reasoning is a kind of counting of markers. We think of all of the individuals that are in the group called "men", and then see how all of these individuals are included in the group called "mortal." Then we note that one of the individuals in the group of men is named "Socrates" and by counting and noting, we can see that the individual Socrates is also in the group called "mortals". This is the process that occurs when we reason.

Errors in Reasoning

The counting and noting functions that are the basis of reasoning are actually quite simple, and given a certain amount of care in performing them, errors should be infrequent. But reasoning can go wrong, and often does. The problem is not in the counting and the noting functions, but in the primary process of labeling. What often happens is that people do not stick consistently to the labels that they began with. This is the problem of equivocation, which for Hobbes was the basic mistake that occurs in faulty reasoning. One begins a sequence of statements using a term that is the label for a certain set of phantasms, but then, especially if the sequence is long and complex, there is a tendency to shift the label to stand for a slightly different set of phantasms. That can lead to very mistaken conclusions. The key to good reasoning then, is consistent definitions. That means that once one has grouped a set of phantasms together and given them a label, one should stick with that label naming that group every time the label comes up in the sequence. If one is consistent in this manner, the reasoning will be correct. Geometry is such a powerful method, because the labels are used consistently. What is called a point or a line in the beginning axioms is not changed, even during long trains of proofs and theorems.

Foundations

With this discussion of materialism, language and reasoning as a background, we are now ready to appreciate the way Hobbes tried to build a geometric-type system concerning human actions that would reveal the causes of war, and would also provide the solutions for peace.   Hobbes' goal was to produce some definitions, and then combine them into sequences of statements that would build to the relevant conclusions. The key to whether this whole process would be successful would be the beginning definitions, for everything else would be based on them.   For Hobbes, the most important definitions were the ones that concern the emotions, that concern peoples' intentions, and that also deal with the beliefs that people have about their situations.   Starting with the proper definitions, Hobbes attempted to use them to form statements that would provide us with an understanding of the problems of war and peace. Furthermore, if these statements are linked in the proper way, then anyone who is rational will have to accept them.

Hobbes' Method of Prudence--The Way of Ordinary Experience

The General Method

But there is a problem, for Hobbes was well aware that not everyone is rational, or at least not everyone has the capacity, the patience or the inclination to follow a long train of complicated arguments. If Hobbes had just been interested in convincing his fellow philosophers of his conclusions, he might not have worried about this issue, but there were actual wars going on including a civil war in his own country. Hobbes wanted to present his views in a way that would be understandable, and then hopefully be acceptable, to all.   This meant that he could not simply use the intellectual way to prove his points, but he would also have to provide a method that was accessible to a wider range of people.

This second lower-level method relied on the experience that every person has whether literate or not, whether philosopher, peasant, courtier or king. This second method is based on our experience, and Hobbes' account of it once again relies on his materialistic view. The objects of the world impinge on our external surfaces, and create a sequence of phantasms inside of us. Furthermore, some of these phantasms cause us to generate other phantasms from our memories. Inspecting this sequence of phantasms we note patterns, and these patterns provide us with data that we use to form expectations about events in the world. In a simple example, we all note the association of dark clouds with rain, and so when we see dark clouds coming toward us, we begin to look around for our umbrellas.

Sometimes, though, the dark clouds appear and then there is no rain. This shows that the way of ordinary experience is not completely reliable. What happens in the past may be a pretty good guide to the future, but it is certainly not a perfect guide. Hobbes thought that the intellectual way was superior, because it was, if done correctly, a much more reliable guide than ordinary experience. Nevertheless, if the intellectual way is one that most people do not use for one reason or another, it is of little value when one wants to convince everyone.

Qualified Introspection

In thinking about matters of war and peace, it is clear that we will have to use the methods available to us to discover some critically important facts about human beings. Using the method of ordinary experience would mean that we should pay attention to the behavior of our species-colleagues and note that often we can detect patterns in them too. When we examine our experience of other people, we can remember that their dark clouds were also followed by rain, thunder and lightening. But again, not always.

However, there is an additional source of experience that a person can use in trying to understand others besides just observing behavior. This additional source is remembering the effects of our own internal states. We can remember various sequences of events that we were involved in ourselves, in which an internal state was the cause of some behavior. For example, I remember a sequence in which I saw an apple on my neighbor's tree, desired to have it, and then made plans to steal it during the night, which I subsequently carried out. I have noted other such sequences in my behavior. Now I see a person watching me in the parking lot of the crowded mall, and trying to make it look like that he is not watching. I have packages in the car. Comparing myself to this other person and making allowances for the difference in circumstances, I can make a pretty good guess about what he is planning to do, and so I lock my car.

This method is one that can be called "qualified introspection" and it is a method for determining what other people are up to. Using oneself as a model, one compares oneself with others, and takes into account the different circumstances and on that basis, tries to determine what the other person is thinking. This is by no means a fool-proof method, as Hobbes clearly realized, but he also thought that it was one of the most useful instruments that we have. In the body of his major work, *Leviathan*, he discusses the intellectual way and the way of ordinary experience in some detail. The method of qualified introspection is presented in the Introduction to the work itself, and Hobbes made a special point of telling his readers at the very beginning that this is the method they should use to verify the claims he was going to make about humanity in his book. Hobbes did not expect that everyone would be able to follow the more intellectual methods that he presented; nevertheless, we can all determine whether what he says is really so. "Read thyself", he says in the Introduction of *Leviathan*, to see if my view of human nature is one that you will agree with.

Questions About the Two Methods

There are a number of questions that can be raised about the usefulness of Hobbes' two methods. Is it really possible to develop an axiomatic system that will yield theorems concerning the causes of war and the solutions for peace? This was Hobbes' dream, but could one ever provide the definitions and axioms that would put a system of this kind on a firm foundation? And aren't there serious questions that can be raised about the view of language and definition that underlies Hobbes' ideas about how such systems are developed? Consider this difficulty in Hobbes' account: he says that definitions are based on the labels that we have provided for a group of "phantasms" among which we have noted a similarity. If this is the way that language develops, then it would certainly seem likely that the definitions of different individuals for the same terms would differ. After all, if the instances of animals that I name 'dog' are quite different than the instances that you have observed and call 'dog', then the meaning of 'dog' for me will be different than it is for you. In that case, how do we actually communicate with language? We each label our particular set of phantasms in our own heads, and I have little reason to believe that my set is anything like your set. Hobbes admitted that experience differs between individuals, and it is experience that serves as the basis for providing the definitions that are the foundation of the axiomatic system.

This leads to another problem. Hobbes tried to distinguish two different methods, one based on language and reason, and the other based on experience. But it is quite obvious that these two methods cannot be distinguished in Hobbes' own terms in the clear-cut way that he attempted. The intellectual way is supposed to be linguistic and rational; the method of ordinary experience is supposed to be available to the less intellectually inclined. But Hobbes himself had to use experience as the basis of providing definitions, and certainly, reasoning would certainly be involved in examining one's own experiences and comparing them to the behavior and actions of others. If there are really two distinct methods involved in Hobbes' theory, then they will have to be described in other terms than the ones that Hobbes used.

There are more difficulties with the way Hobbes set up these methods. Consider again his talk about the phantasms. Given his materialistic views, these phantasms are just combinations of "subtle" particles that have some causal connection to what happens outside of the body. But how is all of this supposed to work? There is some combination of particles in your head, that in a way that is never explained, represent what is going on in the outside world. Even more, how is this combination apprehended so that the person who has it can use it as information for shaping their behavior? A representation, or a map, is only of value if it is perceived. Who is the perceiver? Or doesn't there have to be a perceiver? But if not, then how does that work?

All of the questions raised are difficult and tricky ones, and it is disappointing that Hobbes did not raise them himself. Later philosophers did though, and maybe we should not be too harsh on Hobbes. He was a thinker who was starting a philosophical tradition and he did not have the benefit of relying on the work of many sharp-eyed and sharp-minded philosophers that would keep his distinctions and concepts neat and clean. Later in the 17th and 18th Centuries, many of the points that Hobbes was just beginning to develop coalesced into more definite views about how we develop knowledge-- the Empiricist and Rationalist traditions--one emphasizing experience and the other stressing reason. In Hobbes one can see the original swirls that consolidated into the more definite shapes, but admittedly, these beginning moves by Hobbes are vague, and often, seem to be confused.

Nevertheless, we should not be too eager to disregard what he said as just anticipations of what subsequent thinkers did more cogently. We can see what Hobbes was trying to get at and he does seem to have an important idea. Perhaps the two methods could more usefully be characterized as abstract and concrete. The abstract method relies on broad generalizations and then uses them to deduce particular conclusions. Of course, experience is necessary in developing and verifying the generalizations, but the main goal of this method is to set up a web of relationships between concepts that can be applied to the issues of war and peace. The concrete method, on the other hand, is focussed on reminding people of various experiences that they have had, and then takes these experiences as a basis that people can use to try to determine what other people are likely to think and do. Hobbes thought that both of these methods would yield similar conclusions.

Here is an analogy to illustrate the point of the two methods. Let us say that our car has a tendency to break down and we would like to correct the situation. One way to do this would be by developing concepts of automotive engineering and applying them to this problem. On the basis of this theoretical understanding, we deduce that the problem is with the carburetor. But another thing we might do is to forget about the theoretical stuff, and just try to remember our experience with lousy cars in the past. We might remember our old Chevy and how it coughed and sputtered in a way that is very similar to the behavior of our current car. And what did we do then to fix the problem? We replaced the carburetor and then everything was fine. Maybe if we do the same thing with this car, our problem will also be solved.

Undoubtedly, the abstract method is more powerful than the concrete method, and if done right, will probably yield a more reliable solution. On the other hand, we might not have the time or inclination to learn the necessary concepts of automotive engineering, or we just might not be smart enough to master these ideas. It might well be that the concrete method would provide us with what we need to know to get our car started and to get to work. The abstract method is more reliable and we can be more certain of the results it produces, but the concrete method is more accessible and might be all that we need. Hobbes was interested in the theoretical questions of war and peace, but also in the practical matter of what could be done to stop the disarray that was occurring around him. His two methods contributed to both of these concerns.

The Emotions

The subject of the emotions has obvious relevance to the question of whether people will fight or live in peace. For the most part, Hobbes used the intellectual method in his account of the emotions. He tried to schematize the emotions in a way that would characterize each one as a combination of certain elementary factors. Put the factors together in one way, and the result is anger, but in another combination, the result will be love.

The main factor in understanding the emotions, is the root of the word, 'motion'. Emotions are what move us. The primary factors of motions are direction and velocity. Hobbes called those emotions that move us toward something "appetites" or "desires," and those emotions that make us go away from something were called "aversions."

Another factor in classifying the emotions concerns the object towards which, or away from, we are moving. To illustrate this factor, consider a few examples. Covetousness and ambition are two desires, because they are motions toward something--for covetousness the object is wealth and in the case of ambition, the object is office or precedence. Fear is an aversion because we have the opinion that the object involved will hurt us.

One other factor that should be included in this general scheme is what Hobbes called "delight" and "displeasure." These according to Hobbes are internal motions that accompany our bodily movements caused by whatever emotion we are experiencing. So when we move toward something we think is beneficial, this registers within us as delight, and displeasure is what we experience when we move away from something we consider hostile to us.

These are the basic concepts involved in emotions, and Hobbes believed that he had generated these definitions by means of his intellectual method. Rather than considering whether Hobbes' scheme is complete and valid, what is much more important is how Hobbes used this scheme to make certain general points that set the stage for his main ideas concerning his views about war and peace.

The first point of interest is the way Hobbes defined the concepts of good and evil. 'Good' is the name of any object of desire and 'evil' is the name of an object that we are averse to. What follows from this is that for Hobbes 'good' and 'evil' are terms that vary with the person using them. When we desire some object, we call it "good", but if we are averse to an object, we call it "evil". That is all there is to it according to Hobbes. But what if someone asks whether an object that we all desire is really good? This is an absurd question according to Hobbes. There is no such thing as some object being really good or really evil, for only the desires and aversions of people determine what they call good or evil.

The implications of this view were very provocative in Hobbes' time and they still are, for what he was saying is that he believed that there is no absolute morality. When people say that something is good, all that amounts to is that these people move toward the object. All of the arguments in all the books on philosophy that attempt to prove that goodness is some sort of property that exists in the world apart from our desires are just nonsense. To follow Hobbes' view would mean sweeping several volumes out of the library, but even if we do not accept this point, it does serve to strengthen his account of war and peace. He did not rely on any statements or definitions of morality concerning what is good or bad. People have definite beliefs about morality, but the fact is that these beliefs vary greatly. To avoid this whole issue, Hobbes said, in effect, that in his account he will not rely on any of the moral beliefs that people have. He hoped that would give his view a wider scope of acceptance, for no matter what one thinks of morality, Hobbes did not appeal to it. On his view, there is nothing much to appeal to; nevertheless, moral beliefs have no role in the theory about war.

Another point of great interest is the implication of this account for the question of the constancy and permanence of emotions. Given that this whole view is based on motion, and on the premise that all that exists is matter in motion, the implication is that any individual's emotions will be constantly changing. There will be a never-ending sequence--first an aversion, then a desire, then this, then that. The sequence never stops changing and just rests. What this means is that the fact that someone has a particular emotion on one particular day does not mean that on another day the person would have the same emotion, even in the same external circumstances. Any little difference in the internal states of a person could lead to the person having a different emotion. This presents a serious difficulty in trying to understand others. If I note that someone has moved toward an object in the past, say ice cream, I may think that they will move toward it again in the future. As a matter of fact, because of the existence of different external or internal factors, they may not.

Another very significant point in Hobbes' account concerns our emotions towards things that we do not know. Hobbes said that some of our aversions and appetites are inborn, and some are gained through experience by trying things out and seeing if we like them or not. If we try them and they hurt us, then we will develop an aversion, but what is very significant is that he says we will also have an aversion to those things that we do not know whether they will hurt us or not. What is Hobbes' basis for this claim? Is it a point that follows from the definitions of aversion and knowledge? It does not seem to be. Then it must be based on experience. But Hobbes presented no examples in *Leviathan* at least to support his idea that we are averse to anything that we do not know whether it will hurt us or not. When we think about our own past experience, aren't we often curious about things we don't know? Aren't people adventurous about trying new things? Hobbes might reply we are curious about things we may not have tried personally, but have heard from others that they are worthwhile. This is obviously sometimes true, but there are things no one has ever done before, and some people still plunge into them. Could it be that Hobbes was not simply providing a descriptive statement about this matter, but was providing some advice, about the attitudes it would be smart to have towards things we do not know? This answer is also unsatisfactory because in this part of his theory, he was not attempting to provide any advice to people; that comes later on. Here he was just trying to describe the factors that lead to war. There is no clear answer what the justification is of this point, but nevertheless it played a very crucial part in the theory he was constructing.

One might wonder if this particular point is just a report of Hobbes's own particular suspicious attitudes, and there is some reason to think along this line. Hobbes did say of himself that he was a very fearful person, and he claimed in his verse autobiography, that his mother went into labor in 1588 when she was frightened by accounts of the attack on England by the Spanish Armada. As a result, he said, he and fear were born twins, and that was the reason for his suspicious and fearful nature. He also made a note of stating that when trouble broke out in England, he was the first to flee to the Continent. Even if these stories were true, and if Hobbes was simply doing what many philosophers do--seeing their own reactions as universal ones--we should try to avoid just looking at this point in such a personal way. If Hobbes' ideas are to have any value at all, they have to be more than an account of his own idiosyncrasies. As a matter of fact, this point is crucial to Hobbes' account of war as will be explained below.

Another curious use of the emotion of fear is provided by Hobbes' discussion of religion as he defined religion as a kind of fear. He said that religion is the fear of the unknown and then he says that people make up invisible powers to allay their fears. But, he added that there is such a thing as true religion--when the powers that are imagined actually exist. This is just a definition of what a true religion would be; Hobbes did say that there is any such religion.

Hobbes' views about religion will be considered more extensively later, but this does seem to be a rather curious way to define religion-- not in terms of belief, as it usually is, or as practice and rituals, as it sometimes is. Rather Hobbes saw religion as just a species of fear. Again, this has a very important place in his theory, but one can see why many of Hobbes's contemporaries accused him of being an atheist. This is not the view of religion that would be looked on favorably by most people who actually believe in it.

At the end of his account of the emotions, Hobbes presented his definition of felicity--happiness, and in this case one can see how it does follow from previous points. Given Hobbes' views about the transitory state of all emotions because of the continuous movement of matter, his definition of felicity could not be in terms of some permanent and unchanging state. And as a matter of fact, Hobbes scornfully dismissed any attempt to define happiness in that way. Consistent with his own point of view, Hobbes defined felicity as the continual success in getting what one wants. The picture that he presented is that our desires for the things that we like never end. When we satisfy one desire, another pops up. So we can never be satisfied once and for all, but if we have a pretty good rate of satisfying our desires, then we will be happy, and that is the best that we can hope for.

These are some of the foundational building blocks that Hobbes used to construct his explanation of war, but before leaving the emotions it is worthwhile to note a couple of tangential, but very interesting, points that Hobbes just briefly mentioned in his discussion of the emotions. Hobbes had a richness of mind that could generate ideas about almost any topic, and apparently he did not like to waste any of them, so here and there Hobbes included some material that while perhaps not necessary to the basic issue, is worth considering anyway.

One of his ideas concerns his explanation of laughter. According to him, laughter is like a sudden gust that causes us to convulse, and the cause of this gust is a sudden realization that we did something that pleases ourselves or we noticed some imperfection in another. In other words, we laugh when we think about our own superiority, and often the only way that we can think we are superior, is by demeaning others. This is a somewhat cynical view about laughter, but on reflection and using the method of ordinary experience, it is not that easy to refute. The majority of jokes are funny because they make fun of someone-- their stupidity, their physiques, their vices, or their pretensions. There are no jokes about the virtuous--there is nothing funny about them. And why do we find it so amusing to laugh at others' defects? Hobbes had his interesting explanation.

Another fascinating point is Hobbes' discussion of curiosity. He calls it "the lust of the mind" and says that the search for knowledge, "exceedeth the short vehemence of carnal pleasure." Does this too tell us something about Hobbes and his special proclivities, or did he have a point that is actually based more clearly in general experience than people are accustomed to admitting?

Power

Hobbes' conceptions of the emotions provided some of the most important elements that he used in his account of why people fight, but there is another concept, closely related to his explanation of felicity, that also played a critical role and that is the concept of power. Hobbes said that all of us have a restless desire to increase our power that stops only when we die. It is not that we want money, fame, accomplishment, or knowledge--what we all want is as much power as we can get.

How this view fits what Hobbes had previously said is not difficult to see. Our emotions are turbulent, as they keep providing us with different objects and projects to desire. We want to be happy and that means being able to obtain the objects of our desires. But we can never be sure what it is that we will want. We may get one thing, but we won't rest there, for we are made up of continuing motions and so inevitably, we will want something else. If we cannot get this next thing, we will be frustrated, and then yet another desire will come along to prod us further and if we can't get that one, we will be frustrated even more. In order to protect ourselves from this constant looming frustration, we have to insure ourselves of the means of being able to obtain whatever it is we desire.

We also desire to hold onto what we have. We may have a desire for fame, but no one just wants fifteen minutes. People want continuous fame, and even more, growing fame. This is what leads people to try to increase their power even after they have satisfied some of their desires. Increasing power is not necessary just to get the new things we might want, but also to retain the old things we have already achieved.

Hobbes claimed that the desire for power is not confined to just a few individuals--it is a universal human characteristic. Of course, this desire is expressed in many different ways and Hobbes loved to enumerate the rich variety involved. Even peaceful people, those who would just like cultivate their own gardens and not bother anyone else, desire the power that will enable them to live this sort of life. So it is not just the warriors, the athletes and the vain who are interested in more power. Everyone who has some plan for their life, which for Hobbes meant everyone, wants to have the power that it takes to put this plan into effect, accomplish the aims involved, and then maintain them.

Religion

There is one last element that is needed to complete the set of concepts that Hobbes used to construct his argument concerning the basis of conflict between people. That concept is religion--a concept that Hobbes included in his discussion of the passions, and said was a species of fear. Religion was very important to Hobbes for many reasons, but one of the main ones was that it provided a crucial step in his argument.

Hobbes had to be very careful what he said about religion, because a misstep could lead to very serious consequences. But even though Hobbes claimed to be a fearful and timorous man, he plunged right in and provided a psychological account for the pervasive existence of religion.   Hobbes said that in every culture or group that one investigates, one finds a belief in supernatural entities that are involved in human life. These entities are always invisible. Where does this universal belief come from? What is its source?

The source is the desire for power. We have already concluded that we all desire our power to increase in order to satisfy new desires and hold onto what we already have.   Because we are anxious creatures, we want power as a guarantee to protect us for what may happen in the future. The great cause of our anxiety is that we do not know what the future holds, and so we do not know what problems there will be in increasing our power, or what attacks there will be on it. This makes us nervous, as we try to figure out what is going to happen and then how to shape the future the best way that we can. To allay anxiety about these matters, people invent (not consciously, of course) gods who know the future and who can be appealed to, and this is the source of pagan religion. The ignorant pagans examined animal entrails, looked at the flights of birds, chewed psychodelic leaves and did all sorts of other bizarre things, in order to figure out what signs the gods were sending them about what was going to happen. And then these pagans devised even more bizarre rituals, like killing animals and pouring wine into the ground, in order to assuage the invisible gods and appeal to them to be helpful in increasing the pagans' power. As strange as all of this is, Hobbes thought that the psychological mechanism underlying the rich and amazing variety of religious behavior is simply the anxiety people have about maintaining and increasing their power.   Without the anxiety, there would be no religion.

But what are the implications of all of this for what was considered the true religion--Christianity? This is a very delicate interpretive point. Hobbes declared over and over that he was a Christian, and that he believed that Christianity was the true religion, and that the invisible powers that it asserts really do exist. But he also provided the materials to undercut the sincerity of his own claims of belief in Christianity. If a psychological mechanism can be used to explain the existence of paganism, would it not also apply to Christianity? Hobbes would have said that Christianity is different, because unlike paganism, it is true. Hobbes' contemporaries were unconvinced by his professions of belief, for they thought that his materialism, his reduction of psychological states to the motion of matter, and his general skeptical and ironic attitudes, made it likely that he was actually an atheist. He was so accused many times in his life, and after the Great Fire in London in 1666, some condemned Hobbes for being the cause of it, as God punished Londoners with the fire for letting such an unbeliever live and write among them. For the last twenty years of his life, Hobbes was prohibited from publishing any more philosophy in England. He had to content himself writing translations of some ancient Greek classics.

The Synthesis

The elements are now in place to provide a general explanation why it is that people fight with each other. The elements are the methods we use to develop our ideas about what is going on in the world, the intellectual way and the way of ordinary experience, the definitions of different emotions, the account of power, and the evidence provided by religion. These materials are really quite few--a minimalist toolbox of concepts and points to be arranged and combined to lead to the result that Hobbes wanted to convince us to accept. The minimalism is important, for it means that Hobbes' arguments, if successful, should appeal to many different kinds of people with very different backgrounds. People with different religious views should not be put off by what Hobbes said, because he did not use any religious views in his arguments. The same goes for all the different moral views that people hold. Hobbes abstained from all of these. The question is whether he was able to successfully achieve his goal with these few materials.

Equality

The first point of this synthesis is a startling claim given the time that Hobbes was writing. This claim is that all people are equal by nature. Hobbes wrote this statement more than a century before the

American Revolution and its basic document that would claim that "all men are created equal". Also he was writing in England and Europe, in countries containing nobles, aristocrats, lords and peasants, where class divisions were very distinct and obvious in daily life. Finally, Hobbes wrote that all 'men' are by nature equal, and not all 'people' are equal, but an examination of his argument reveals no particular male bias, and nothing would be changed in his account if he had used more gender-neutral language.

Even more startling is the sense in which Hobbes said that people are equal. Whenever someone claims that humans are equal, it always raises the question in what respect, because there are obvious differences between people. Hobbes said that all people are equal in two respects--strength and quickness of mind. But this seems to be manifestly preposterous. People are equal in strength--does this mean that anyone of us can be compared to Arnold Schwarzenegger? And we are also equal in quickness of mind? What could he have meant by this?

Hobbes gave each one of these points a very unique twist. As far as physical strength goes, we are all equal because the weakest can kill the strongest. No one is invulnerable. Mr. Schwarenegger is a mighty specimen all right, but he has to sleep, and when he does, he is as vulnerable as anyone else. Even when he is awake, with all of his muscles, he cannot repel the bullet of a small hand-gun. All of us have our moments when we are not alert, and all of us are covered by very soft and permeable armor. Anyone can be hit from behind, and that includes the most powerful political authorities that command vast armies. This is the peculiar sense in which Hobbes said we are equal in strength. We are all equally vulnerable to being attacked, and the weakest can kill the strongest.

The argument for the equality of quickness of mind is more complicated and is also harder to accept. He said that quickness of mind involves the facility people have in using the two methods, the intellectual way and the way of ordinary experience. Since the intellectual way is so rarely used, it can just be dismissed, and that means that the relevant method for this point is the way of ordinary experience. But here there is obviously equality, for everyone piles up experience at the same rate, one experience a second or something like that. He also threw in the observation that the only reason that people do not think people are equal in quickness of mind is because they over-rate themselves, but the real proof that this particular capacity is equally distributed is that everyone is satisfied with their share.

It is at points like this that it is sometimes difficult to understand Hobbes, because what he was saying seems to be so irrelevant to the point he is trying to make, or else so poorly argued. For example, even if everyone piles up experiences at an equal rate, some people still will have more experiences than others just because they are older. Another point--even if everyone is satisfied with their share, it does not at all follow that the shares are equally distributed. Was Hobbes just making foolish mistakes here, or is there some underlying point that is really worth considering?

If we read Hobbes generously, we can see what he is getting at. People generally do trust their cognitive abilities in the sense that they think they have enough of them to get what it is that they want. When people get frustrated, it is very rare that they blame their own abilities to figure things out. Rather, it is much more common to attribute the problem to circumstances, fate, or other evil people. Thus, Hobbes' point can be recast into the view that most people are confident enough in themselves to think that when they act, they can get what it is that they desire. This can also be seen as a minimalist point that would be difficult for anyone to deny. When people have a desire, they generally believe that they have the capacity to do what is necessary to satisfy it. This is an important point in Hobbes' theory, and stated in this general way, it is not very controversial.

Suspicion

Our human situation consists of living near a number of other individuals, who all have desires that they think they can satisfy. The difficulty arises when it becomes clear that there are scarce resources and that for one person to be satisfied, another will have to lose. In the simplest of cases, this is clearly true. If one person wants to possess a physical object and use it when she wants, and another person has the same desire, then neither of the two can satisfy their desires at the same time. But, one might object, couldn't the two share the object? There are grave problems with sharing and Hobbes' basic concepts and premises provide the materials to construct an explanation of why this is so.

First, no one really wants to share. It is always a compromise. The best situation that we all want would be one where we could have the object to ourselves. However, that is not always possible, so if we do not want to fight for possession of the object, we have to share. But sharing can only take place when we can trust that the other person will not take advantage. Sharing is based on an agreement, but the question is how do we know that the other person will not try to cheat on the agreement. Given the premise about the desire for power, we have reason to think that the other person also wants sole possession. Even so, it is possible that the other is an honorable person who will keep to the agreement to share. However, we cannot really know whether the other person is honorable or not, and since we do not know, we are suspicious of them. And this suspicion leads us to treat them in a certain way--maybe to cheat on them before they cheat on us. Of course, the other person may be thinking the same things about us--an implication of Hobbes' claim that people are equal in their quickness of mind. And since we know that they may be thinking this way about us, and therefore may not trust us, then it might be a good idea to strike first. Suspicion thus leads to conflict.

There are two things that would modify this problematic situation. The first is that there would be enough goods so that no one would need to share and everyone could have what they wanted. The second one would be that we could tell if the other person was really trustworthy or not. But unfortunately, neither of these conditions exists.

Scarcity

If we lived in the Garden of Eden where everyone could just pick what was wanted off the nearest tree, then one major source of conflict would be avoided. But even though there has been a material explosion since Hobbes' time, we are still very far from paradise. Nature and technology are still quite stingy in what they provide for us. The commodities we need still cost money--there is no free lunch or free anything else, and that means that there is competition for material goods. When everything is free, we will know that there is enough so that competition will be unnecessary. That is not our situation, nor will it occur for as long as we can foresee.

But even if the material scarcity could be overcome, there is another kind of scarcity that would still plague us. People not only compete for material goods, according to Hobbes, they also compete for honor. People want to be esteemed, and esteem on his view is a necessarily scarce good. One can have Utopian fantasies about solving the problem of the scarcity of material goods, but the desire for esteem can never be solved for everyone, because not everyone can have high self-esteem. We get our esteem by winning competitions with others, and it is a logical truth that everyone cannot be a winner. Even children in kindergarten realize that when everyone receives a blue ribbon for their artwork, the blue ribbon means nothing, and they all want to know whose work is really the best. We all desire honor, glory, self-esteem and reputation, but it is an unfortunate fact that the nature of these goods is that they are brutally and necessarily scarce. For us to get our glory, we will have to be better than others, and it would help if the others would admit it. But the others want their glory too, and they see us as standing in their way. So, for us to get what we want, we have to defeat them, and for others to satisfy their desires, they have to defeat us. Scarcity leads to conflict.

Skepticism about human nature

Was Hobbes saying that everyone wants glory, honor, and reputation and would be willing to fight for it? Was he also saying that people are never willing to share, and they would always fight before sharing? If this was his view, he was certainly mistaken, for certainly this is a simplification of the variety of humankind. There are people who seem to be satisfied with a modest lot, and there are people who not only share, but who are generous and give things away. Maybe even on occasion, we ourselves have been modest and giving. So what should we say about this point of Hobbes? This is another point at which we have to either to dismiss Hobbes' view as being too simple-minded for serious consideration, or else we can be generous and look deeper, and try to see whether some plausible point can be developed from what Hobbes said.

In Hobbes' account of human nature, he does emphasize the aspects of people that could be called egotistical. He especially emphasized these aspects in the earlier forms of his theory. In an earlier work, Hobbes said that we associate with each other just for gain or glory. In an even earlier work Hobbes said that life is a race to excel one's neighbors, and as long as one is ahead, one is happy. But as Hobbes became older, he became more circumspect, and while he did like to dwell on the self-interested aspects of human nature, he also provided the basis of an argument that led to the conclusion that we do not really know each other very well. This conclusion is a skeptical one about human nature--we do not know the aims and motives of other people with any definite reliability.

Skepticism in general

Hobbes lived most of his life in the 17th Century, a century in which there was a great revival in interest in skepticism. Skepticism is the philosophical view that we do not have knowledge. A total skeptic would claim that we do not know anything. This is a difficult argument to make because what premises could be used to establish it? More limited forms of skepticism assert that knowledge is lacking in some particular domain.

Rene Descartes, one of Hobbes' contemporaries, and a figure of great importance in the history of philosophy of this period, was greatly concerned with skepticism as were many of Hobbes' other contemporaries. There were a number of reasons why skepticism became of such great interest at this time. We are used to the swift change of beliefs and practices, but the pace of change in the past was much slower. For example, for several centuries in Europe, there had been one main religious authority, the Catholic Church, and for the great majority of people, the Church's view was the truth on anything that was of importance. But shortly before Hobbes' birth, Martin Luther appeared on the scene and challenged the authority of the Catholic Church. He said that it was not necessary to believe the Church on many matters. We live now at a time when challenging a religious authority on some particular issue is a common occurrence, but in the 17th Century this kind of challenge was considered amazing, and very upsetting. It led to all sorts of squabbles and even to wars, but another effect of the Protestant challenge was to cause serious people to wonder whether the truth about the ultimate questions could ever be known. It was no longer the case that everyone accepted the Catholic Church as the religious authority. Could it be that there was no authority in religion, and that perhaps, no one really has knowledge in these matters?

Another event that contributed to the development of skepticism in the 17th Century was the Copernican Revolution. Again, it takes a bit of imagination to put ourselves into the mind-set of that past time. When we think about it, what could be more obvious than that the earth stands still? How could anyone doubt it? First, there is the evidence of our senses. We see the sun moving, rising in the East and setting in the West. The ground under our feet clearly does not feel like it is moving at a rate of a thousand miles an hour. What could be more stable and unmoving than the earth? And yet, in spite of all this, it does move, and everything that our senses tell us about the stability of the earth is just an illusion.

There were also learned arguments about why the earth must be still. The idea that the earth may be moving had been considered, but it had been rejected for the following reasons. If the earth were moving, there would be a big wind all of the time. There is no such constant wind. If the earth were spinning, objects would fly off of it. Objects rest quite easily on the earth's surface. Finally, if the earth were moving, then if one dropped an object at eye-level, it would not fall straight down. But objects do fall straight down.

All of these arguments seem reasonable enough, and yet they turned out to be mistaken too. And so, the support of the senses and reason turned out to be unreliable concerning a fact about the world that would seem to be very obvious. If our senses and reason cannot provide us with reliable information on the matter of the movement of the earth, how can they be trusted for anything? In the 20th Century, we are completely convinced that the earth moves, but who knows if that also will not turn out to be a mistake?

The challenges to the established religion, and also to the established science led to a growing interest in skepticism. Also the skeptical arguments of Sextus Empiricus, a philosopher who lived in the 3rd Century A.D. were rediscovered after having been lost to Europe for centuries. These arguments were just more logs to add to the growing skeptical firestorm.

Skepticism about human nature again

Hobbes was part of the intellectual community that was very taken with skepticism, and it played a role in his thinking too. But he was not inclined to develop the total skeptical view that was of such enormous interest to Descartes and others. Hobbes was more of a limited skeptic and was interested in the question of how well we can know what our fellow human beings are up to. That is the critical question for living with them, even more important than the factor of scarcity. While scarcity will always mean that there will be some conflict between our own desires and those of others, the conflict involved need not reach the stage of fighting. We could always work out a sharing arrangement, or else we could perhaps understand the other person well enough to know just how far we can impede their desires before they will fight. Scarcity only leads to conflict when we do not know what other people are planning and how intensely they will pursue their desires.

This means that the critical question is, how well do we know other people. While almost everyone has a tale or two of betrayal by someone we thought we knew, is this kind of thing so common? Can nobody be trusted?

Since Hobbes provided us with two methods for finding answers, we can see if either one of them would be useful in finding the critical information we need about other people. The intellectual way does not seem to be of much help. This method provides theoretical abstract kind of knowledge, that while interesting, is not going to really tell us whether our particular neighbors are plotting against us to exclude us from the block party. We are much more likely to find out the kind of information we need by using the method of ordinary experience. This method is based on the capacity that everyone has, unlike the intellectual way that Hobbes said only a few people can actually use. In using the method of ordinary experience to answer this question, we have a running start that we might not have if we used it with other topics. This advantage is our own passions and desires. We can look at our own desires and see on what occasions we had them, and use that as a basis for determining what other people want, and how far they would go to satisfy their desires. We might remember when we were in line and someone butted in, and how we felt and how we acted, and so that provides us with a clue of how others will act when we are inclined to butt in.

But of course, this method also has its problems. One is that the method becomes less reliable the more different the circumstances are between when we acted and the situation that we are now facing. If the circumstances were identical, then we can be quite confident that the result would be the same. But they never are identical, and sometimes not even close. Another problem is that people have the capacity to deceive us, both with words and gestures. They can act just like we did on some occasion when we were promising to meet someone, and they can even say the same words, but hidden behind the outward words and acts, is an intention to break the promise. While we may be just material objects, we still possess an inside as well as an outside, and the outside may not be a very good indicator of what phantasms are occurring on the inside. Thus, the method of ordinary experience is not very reliable when we apply it to the aims and desires of other people.

What this leads to is the conclusion that we do not have any reliable way to know whether other people can be trusted. We cannot really use the intellectual way to determine what others are thinking at a particular time, and the method of ordinary experience cannot tell us either what others desire or what they are thinking. But ordinary experience can reveal to us that in fact, we are not confident about our knowledge of others. We constantly are protecting ourselves by locking our doors. We know that there are police who will punish thieves and still we worry about the safety of our persons and property. We even lock our most important writings and documents in cabinets in our own houses, to protect them against the prying eyes of people we know best. We cannot be sure about what they will do. We do not know enough about other people to know whether they are trustworthy or not, and our actions express this all of the time.

Suspicion Again

Since we cannot be sure about what others are up to, and since we cannot identify those who will seriously interfere with our power, it is not surprising that we would have an attitude of suspicion, and that it will apply to everyone. Who knows in which hearts evil lurks? We had better be careful, very careful. We had better adopt a defensive posture, and be ready at all times to protect ourselves. We might even consider the wisdom of some pre-emptive attacks--get them before they get us. Of course, others are in the same position we are in, and this means that they will be thinking the same way. They will be suspicious of us. They will also be thinking of making pre-emptive attacks. But we don't know that they are thinking this way, but they certainly might be. This makes us even more suspicious and more likely to attack first. The vicious descending spiral is only too obvious, and as the suspicions build up, the likelihood of attack becomes greater. Unless something is done, we will all be living in a state of war that will be awful. This is the source of his famous phrase that in this kind of state, life will be "solitary, poor, nasty, brutish and short."

This state of constant war can clearly be seen in the relationship between countries. Every country has a Department of Defense and an army, ready to defend and attack. This does not express a very optimistic view of the neighboring countries. Often this Department of Defense has weapons that could very easily be used to attack another country first--in fact, they are poised and ready to do so. A pre-emptive strike is not necessarily aggressive; it can actually be a defensive tactic. To be sure it would be difficult to distinguish it from an aggressive first strike, and there may not be any good reason to make this distinction. Every country is suspicious of other countries and waits armed and ready to repel invasions. Any country that sees a neighbor assuming a suspicious posture quickly concludes that they had better make the same preparations. Even if war does not break out immediately, the atmosphere is hostile, and it will not take much to begin the shooting.

Brief summary

The beginning point of Hobbes' viewpoint on war is that people have desires. However, the objects for satisfying these desires are scarce, because of the nature of the physical world and because some of the things we desire just cannot be shared. In spite of these obstacles, human beings strive to increase their power to attain the satisfaction of their desires, and since all people are doing the same thing, competition ensues.

This competition could be mediated if we could judge to what extent others would be willing to compromise on the pursuit of their desires, but we cannot reliably judge this matter about other people. We cannot tell if we can trust others to share or to agree to inhibit their desires, and so lacking this crucial knowledge of others, we are suspicious of them.   This suspicion leads to us taking a defensive posture toward each other and even contemplating pre-emptive actions. Given all of these factors, conflict and war are inevitable.

Discussion of the synthesis

In looking at these main points in the summary of Hobbes' argument, it is interesting to note what changes would lead to less conflict. Clearly, if the world were more abundant, there would be less reason for war. If we lived in a Garden of Eden where everything we wanted, TV's and Twinkies, grew on trees and just had to be picked, then one reason for fighting would be eliminated. But unfortunately, the world is stingy with us, and we have to work and labor to get the things we desire.

Another factor that leads to conflict is the presence of so many others--all of these people with their grasping desires, just like us. If there were fewer, or maybe no others at all, we might be better off. And then there is the strength of peoples' desires. If people would just give in more and be satisfied with just a little, there would be less conflict. But peoples' desires are strong and demanding, and so many are unsatisfied with just half a loaf.

Finally, the most critical factor in this whole account is that we cannot reliably judge what other people are up to. Maybe this view of Hobbes is exaggerated and it does not apply to everyone.   But it definitely applies to some.   There are clearly some people who are untrustworthy and the problem is that we have trouble identifying those who would take advantage of us. If they just had some mark, we could avoid them, or the rest of us (for surely, _we_ are trustworthy) could band together in mutual protection organizations, but the nightmare of the situation is that we cannot pick out the deceivers. So even if Hobbes' view is not universally true and everyone is not a demanding and devious non-compromiser, it definitely is true of some people. Combining this point with the fact that we cannot identify the nasties means there will be suspicion of everyone.   Once the suspicion starts developing, it is difficult to stop it. Any look, any little move, can begin the motions that will lead to the malignant and consuming whirlpool that will drown everyone.

Assessment of the Synthesis

The point of Hobbes' synthesis is to provide the definitive answer to why it is that people fight. This is why we can't just get along together. We are suspicious of each other, and for good reason. When we are in a situation where we cannot trust others, the result will be conflict and war.

As an account of the conflicts between countries, Hobbes' theory can be substantiated with innumerable examples. Countries compete for limited space, for scarce resources, and for glory and honor, which are necessarily limited. Every war can be traced to one of these causes. Furthermore, even when there is no hot war going on, countries are suspicious of each other and keep an armed guard at a hair-trigger state of readiness.

But is Hobbes' claim true for all countries and at all times? What about the border of Canada and the United States--thousands of miles long and not one tank or machine gun to be seen? This is not the only case of friendly relations between countries. How would Hobbes explain that?

A Hobbsian response to this objection could take the following form. Unlike human individuals, who are relatively equal, countries can vary greatly in their comparative strength and capacities. In some cases, one country will be overwhelmingly stronger and more powerful than its neighbor. When a situation of this type occurs, there really is no competition between the parties and they can live in peace. The weaker country is over-awed by the stronger. The stronger knows that it is immune to attack from the weaker. As a result there is no conflict.

But consider what happens when the strengths and capacities of two countries are similar. Then there will be trouble. Then the never-ending suspicion and mistrust begin. Then each one begins to wonder what the other is up to, and the deadly dialectic begins. The case for Hobbes, at least at the country level, is very strong.

But does his argument also apply to individuals? At this level the contending parties are equal in the relevant ways that Hobbes set out. But is every individual mistrustful and suspicious, or is this a view that is just the product of a seriously paranoid mind?

There is plenty of evidence to support Hobbes' main contention about the sources of conflict. Of course, not all of us are constantly on guard against each other, but it is the rare person who goes through their whole life without being surprised by someone they thought they knew very well, and often the surprise is a nasty one. The fact is that as a species we are expert deceivers, and while we have developed some high-grade deceit-detectors, they do not work perfectly. In our business lives we insist on contracts. In our personal lives we engage in marriages--another kind of contract. These contracts are enforceable--if one party does not comply, there is a penalty. This provides us with some confidence about others, but even with that people do not always do what they say they will do. Yes, trust is nice, but make sure the other signs on the dotted line. Even with a signature, be careful. Anything less is naive.

3
PEACE

The Solution--Creating a Sovereign

But all is not lost. There is a solution. Two factors in human nature incline us towards the solution. The first is the passion of fear and the second is reason.

First, fear. Fear is the passion that we have already seen is powerful and universal. While Hobbes used skepticism about other people as a very important part of his argument about war, his skepticism was limited. We can know that people fear death and wounds, and are very anxious about their futures. The universality of religion is the evidence for that. While it is true that humans are competitive and desirous and are constantly seeking power, at some point fear kicks in especially when they realize, as they sometimes do, that the current course is going to lead to disaster. Disaster is something that we all fear, and eventually people are capable of seeing it as the likely result of where we are headed.

But what can we do? How do we get out of the predicament where everyone is suspicious of everyone else? Reason comes to the rescue. It is not completely clear just what Hobbes meant by reason at this point in his argument, but the general point he was making is quite evident. He meant that we are capable of generating arrangements and ideas that will get us out of this trouble. It is one thing to think of a solution, and quite another to actually have the drive and energy needed to put it into practice. Reason, at least, can make suggestions, but again the passions will be needed to move us to the desired result.

The Prescriptive Aspect of the Solution

Hobbes' account of war and conflict was a structure built on certain basic elements. In developing his view concerning the solution to conflict, Hobbes again tried to provide a minimalist account--one that would just use uncontroversial notions that would convince anyone, no matter what other moral, religious or political view they held. But there is also an important difference between his solution for peace and the account of war. In telling us why people fight, Hobbes was presenting a descriptive theory. He was not really offering any advice in that part; he was just stating what the factors are that lead to conflict. The account of the solution is different, because Hobbes was not just describing how people come to be peaceful. On this matter he was an advocate. He wanted to convince people that there is a way to get to peace, and that it is something they should adopt. Further, he thought his solution was the only one that is likely to work, and since he was living in a very turbulent time of civil war, he thought it was urgent that people adopt his proposal. To evaluate Hobbes' solution, it will no longer be sufficient for us to just observe, record and verify whether Hobbes' statements are accurate representations of humanity. His solution is a prescription of what we must do to save ourselves. We now only have to ask ourselves whether what he is saying is true, but we also have to consider whether his advice is worthwhile.

The Artificial Aspect of the Solution

For Hobbes there was another striking difference between war and peace which is that war is natural, but peace is an artificial contrivance. (Is it a relevant fact that whenever we mention this pair, we always mention war first?) For Hobbes war is our natural state, and we have to use our ingenuity to figure out how to defeat nature. In having this view, Hobbes realized that he was disagreeing with the foremost philosophical authority of the ages--Aristotle, who was known for centuries as The Philosopher. It was Aristotle who was the given the place of honor among philosophers in the Middle Ages, even though he was a pagan. When Hobbes went to college at Oxford, it was

Aristotle's works that were studied, and what Aristotle had to say was seldom questioned.

Hobbes, however, as part of the development of new ideas in the 17th Century, vehemently rejected Aristotle, and in almost every reference to Aristotle, the Hobbsian gifts of vituperation and insult are most apparent. Hobbes found one doctrine of Aristotle's to be particularly mistaken, and that is the view that humans are political animals. For Aristotle, we associate with each other and form communities as part of our nature. We are not solitary creatures, for in Aristotle's view, a human who wants to live alone is either a god or a beast. Hobbes did not necessarily think that we have the natural desire to be hermits, but he also did not think that we are political and social by nature. Bees and ants may be social animals, but human are not. Cattle and wolves may live together without any special contrivance, but humans do not.

Hobbes discussed this question of whether human beings are social by nature in all three versions of his political philosophy, and in each case, he provided six reasons to disprove Aristotle's views. In each account the main reason we are different from the social animals is because we have reason and speech that they lack. Reason and speech provide each individual with the capacity to consider what their own private good is as opposed to the common good, and this leads to a variety of different views which leads to conflict and war.

Hobbes was by no means an eminent zoologist, and there is no evidence that he made a careful study of animals, but there is a point to what he was saying, although it may be better expressed in different terms than he used. Humans are different than the other social animals because our behavior is less stereotyped than theirs. We have more developed capacities for pretending and deceiving, and speech and reason are the main tools we use for this purpose. For example, when wolves are establishing a system of dominance in their packs, there are various behaviors they go through in order to determine who will be the leader. These behaviors are standard and ritualized, and once established tend to be stable, at least for a while. But things are not so set for us humans. We plot, we lie, we intrigue, we deceive, and we are often unsatisfied. Consider any drama or history about the court of a monarch. Everyone has their own private agenda, and there are shifting and changing conspiracies that rival the movements of the Sahara in a windstorm. And what happens in the courts of monarchs can be seen in every office, factory, and family. We spend an inordinate amount of time trying to figure out who is plotting what, and who is being honest with us. But since our behavior is not very stereotyped, we cannot really be sure if others are sincere or if they are just pretending. Once again it is our inability to know what others are up to that is the significant factor. It is main reason why we cannot just be social animals like bees and ants. We do not know each other well enough to have the easy cooperation that some animals have. For us, cooperation is something we have to construct, for it does not come naturally.

Basic Concepts

Liberty, Right and Law

In presenting his solution to our predicament, Hobbes once again tried to present his view in a systematic way. This again meant that he would have to start with definitions, and organize them into propositions that would lead to his desired conclusions. In this way he hoped to provide an argument that would be clear and would convince everyone who would be willing to pay attention to it.

The first definition Hobbes provided was that of liberty. Hobbes had a very simple, straightforward definition for liberty. A person has liberty to the extent that there are no external obstacles standing in the way of what the person is trying to obtain. Complete liberty would mean that the person could obtain anything desired. Maybe Adam and Eve came as close to complete liberty as we can imagine. In the Garden of Eden they could just take what was there. There was only one limit--the fruit of that special tree.

Liberty is the basis of the definition of the next concept--the concept of a natural right. Our natural rights, according to Hobbes, consist in the liberty that we have to use our power in any way we think is necessary to preserve our own life. This is not a right that we are given by anyone or by any institution. What Hobbes meant is that we are creatures, born with desires to get what we need to preserve ourselves, and that is what we will actually do. We will try to overcome any obstacles in our way to accomplish goal of staying alive. Whatever we determine is necessary to do to survive, we will do. This is the kind of situation that Hobbes called, exercising our natural rights.

The use of the term 'right' can be confusing, because usually this term is related to some document or governmental decision. Thus, we have the Bill of Rights of the Constitution which states that the government of the United States will not erect obstacles that will hinder the citizens of the country from performing various activities, such as saying what we want, associating with people of our choice, etc. When

Hobbes talked about natural rights, he was not talking about what some official body says that we can do; rather, he was talking about what we can do as creatures with desires. Before we become citizens of a state that we invent, we are creatures trying to do our best to satisfy our desires.

The third basic concept is that of a law of nature. While rights are defined in terms of liberties, laws are defined in terms of the opposite of liberties--restrictions. Rights are what we can do; laws are what we should refrain from doing. The rights of nature are what we deem necessary for our own preservation. The laws of nature forbid us from doing those things that will lead to our destruction.

Four Other Basic Concepts--Contracts, Laying Down Rights, Covenants and Free Gifts

When Hobbes defined the terms 'right of nature' and 'law of nature' he did not think we should just look around to see whether his definitions are correct. These terms are very unlike the concepts he defined earlier when he was discussing the causes of war. In the previous case the main concepts were fear, desire, good, bad, etc. and these are terms that we all use, and so we can see if what Hobbes said corresponds with our own usage. But we do not talk about rights and laws of nature, and so another approach is necessary to understand this part of Hobbes' theory.

Hobbes claimed that everyone has the right of nature to everything. By saying this, he was not reporting or describing human actions, but rather it is more helpful to see him as presenting a useful picture. The picture is of a collection of human beings scattered on an isolated island. Each one of these humans wants to live, and each one will do what is necessary to achieve that goal. Each one will try to take whatever food is available, will take the materials needed for shelter, and if these objects are in the proximity of another person, each one will use stealth or strength to obtain them. No one, in this situation, will acknowledge any restrictions on what they can take. In this picture, each individual has the natural right to everything on the island--which means that they will take what they think is necessary to maintain their own lives.

Of course, we have seen that this kind of situation will lead to war, conflict and general nastiness, and so the individuals will try to think of ways to make their situation better. The obvious one is for them to make a contract with each. It would really improve things if the people on the island made an agreement where they consent to not rob or steal from each other, and perhaps even to share in the necessities of life.

Hobbes had an interesting account of just what it means to make such a contract. In his account, what is involved in a contract is called "the laying down of a right." What this means is that a person gives up the natural right they have to everything and states the intention to not interfere with someone else exercising their natural right to everything. In laying down a right, it is not necessary that the person give up their rights to everything, for we may just lay down rights to some specific object. Also, we do not just lay down our rights for the fun of it, but we do this because we hope to obtain some benefit thereby for ourselves. In most cases the laying down of rights is mutual. One person gives up their right to something, and someone else gives up their right to something else, and the result is an exchange that helps both parties.

For example, person A on the island has collected twenty-five coconuts, but realizes that he cannot eat all of them before they become spoiled. Person B has made several cutting instruments out of stones, but also realizes that he cannot use all of them. So A lays down the right he has to all the coconuts and tells B that he will not interfere with B exercising the right B already has over the coconuts. And B does the same thing with some of his cutting instruments. Each one says that they will not interfere with the other one's rights to some particular objects. They both lay down their rights that they had to these objects, and so a contract and an exchange is made.

This is the basic form of all contracts according to Hobbes. Every contract specifies that each party lay down their natural right to some thing. This is the same form that is involved in contracts between people where one buys the services of another. The buyer lays down their right to part of their money and will not interfere with the other's appropriation of it. The person providing the service lays down their right to the use of their own body for a specific amount of time and will do what the buyer demands.

There are two variations of the concept of the contract that also were very important for Hobbes. The first of these concepts is that of a covenant. A covenant is a contract where one or both of the parties agrees to lay down their rights in the future. In a contract both parties lay down their rights simultaneously, but this is not so in a covenant. Most of the contracts that people actually make are covenants in Hobbes' terms. We agree to work now, and the employer agrees to pay us later. A marriage is an interesting covenant in which Hobbes would say each party lays down their right to pursue other individuals. The main feature of covenants is trust, because at least one of the parties has to trust that the other one will do in the future what they said they would do. There is no immediate tit for tat. This focuses the issue on what is the critical problem of peace--how can we create trust when we have so much reason to be suspicious.

The second variation of the contract is a free-gift. In this case, only one of the parties lays down a right. The other party does nothing. So when we give a tie as a birthday present to a friend, we renounce our natural right to the tie. The friend can exercise his right to own it, wear it, give it away, throw it out, or use it as a tourniquet. But the recipient of the gift does not lay down any of his rights, and this raised the question why anyone would make a free-gift according to Hobbes. To explain free gifts, Hobbes relied on his view of universality of self-interest. We give gifts in the hope of getting someone's friendship, to maybe enhance our own reputation, to gain rewards in heaven or to free our mind "from the pain of compassion." Hobbes did not suggest we might give gifts just to make someone else happier.

The Way to Achieve Peace

The elements are now in place for presenting Hobbes' solution for achieving peace. The solution is that people should make a contract with each other to give up their natural rights to everything. The concept of natural rights, combined with our passions, the scarcity of resources and our inability to understand others lead to conflict and war. We see that, and we also see, by means of our reason, the way to stop the war. We have to make an agreement to limit our exercise of our natural rights if others will do so too. It is really as simple as that. In the agreement in which we stop the war, we also create the laws of morality that forbid killing, stealing and slandering. It is not necessary to say that God wants us to obey these laws. We can see ourselves that we have to give up our right to kill and take from others if we are to avoid living awful lives and ultimately being destroyed. Hobbes called this realization a law of nature--a restriction our reason tells us that we must apply to ourselves, as long as everyone else does so too, in order to achieve peace. While we may not be naturally peaceful creatures, we do have the capacity of reason that tells us how to end our conflicts. Reason tells us to make agreements, to establish laws, to enact restrictions, to bind ourselves to these laws and restrictions, and thus to create duties and obligations for ourselves. Reason tells us, in other words, to create moral rules that will lead to our own preservation.

A Complication

Unfortunately, it is not all that simple. The agreement that has to be made becomes very tricky to carry out, and Hobbes almost seemed to take delight in raising problems and complications concerning this basic agreement that establishes society. Here is one problem. Hobbes said that covenants made in the state of nature are void. To see what this means, let us suppose that two people on our island have wearied of the constant fighting and conflict and have decided to lay down their rights and make an agreement with each other that they will not take the other's food anymore. This agreement would be a covenant because it involves future behavior. However, Hobbes said that this kind of covenant would be invalid, because it is based on trust, and neither party has any basis for trusting the other. Oh yes, the other person said that they will honor the agreement, but Hobbes was not impressed with the mere utterance of some sentence. It is too easy to lie, or to change one's mind when it becomes advantageous. Also, neither person can really tell whether the other person will honor the contract just by looking at them and remembering past actions. Peoples' actions can be as deceptive as their words, and also there is the old mutability issue-- that while a person may sincerely intend to keep an agreement today, the rush and swirl of the particles and phantasms can lead to very different intentions and desires tomorrow. We cannot be sure the other will live up to the agreement, and then why should we, and then why not get them before they get us, and off we go.

This complication is intriguing and important in itself, but it also points to the main issue for Hobbes. Suspicion is the cause of war, and trust is what is needed for peace, but how can the trust be created? It is not a natural faculty for people to trust each other; it has to be created and for Hobbes that meant that it is artificial. But how does one create trust? How can we have confidence that the other person will keep their part of a covenant--that they will lay down their right in the future?

A Proposed Solution to the Complication

The solution is to create a power, a terrifying power that will enforce the agreements. This terrifying power will punish those who do not keep their covenant. With such a power in force, we can have the requisite confidence in other people. But if there is no such power, all covenants are invalid.

The key mechanism in this whole business is fear. People will not keep their covenants unless they are afraid that breaking the covenant will be disadvantageous for them. So we can trust others when we know that if they break their word, they will suffer some very severe penalty--something that they would certainly be afraid of happening to them. But this kind of trust depends upon our confidence that first, there is such a power, and second, that everyone would actually be afraid of it. Considering the second question, is there reason to believe that fear is that universal among people. We have already shown that it is, as the universality of religion is the key point of evidence. The existence of religion, according to Hobbes, indicated that people are afraid of what will happen to them. This is one point where he did not invoke skepticism about other people. If we did not know that everyone was afraid, there would be no solution to the problem. So at least we can know this much about our fellow species-members--they will adjust their behavior to avoid what they are afraid of.

Creating the Fearful Power--The Sovereign

The main question is how do we create a fearful power that will make people keep their agreements. We can do this by agreeing with each other, that we shall all lay down our rights, and then just let some individual, or some group, have all of the power over us. The person or group for whom we lay down our rights, will have the right to do anything they want, and we will not be able to interfere with them.

To illustrate this point, let us return to the island and imagine that we are among the individuals on it. We all can see that we will soon die if we do not do something to institute peace. Several individuals have already made weapons for their defense, and of course, these weapons can be used for attack too. There is only one possibility for us to get out of this predicament. We have to agree to give up our rights to just take what we want and need, but more importantly, we have to give up our weapons. But still there needs to be some way to enforce the agreement. To this end, we also agree to let one person, let us call him Mighty Joe, not be party to this agreement and that means that he will have all of the weapons we have given up. We say, "Mighty Joe, you will be the leader as we give you the power to rule us, to set the laws, and to enforce agreements. By giving up our weapons, we have made ourselves defenseless, and that means you can punish us in any way you see fit if we violate any of the laws you will set up".

Now Mighty Joe is armed to the teeth, and we have nothing, but Mighty Joe has not really gained any rights that he did not previously possess. It is just that we have agreed not to get in his way. Mighty Joe is now a terrifying and overwhelming force, compared to us, and he even has the power to kill us. In Hobbes' terms, Mighty Joe is the sovereign, and we are the subjects.

Before raising the obvious questions about the wisdom of granting Mighty Joe so much power, let us first consider some of the implications that Hobbes drew from his view about how the sovereign was created. It is important to note that the Mighty Joe himself was not a party to the agreement. We did not make an agreement with him, that we will obey his laws and rules as long as he does his part in enforcing our agreements. No such agreement would be possible according to Hobbes because once we have given him our weapons, there is no power to make sure that Mighty Joe keeps his part. So rather than us making an agreement with him, we are actually just making it with each other. That means, according to Hobbes, we can never protest that Mighty Joe is not keeping his word, or that he is not doing what he is supposed to do. Mighty Joe made no promises, made no agreements, and so there is no basis for any complaint.

Suppose that only a majority of us agreed to make Mighty Joe the sovereign. There are some individuals who decided that they did not want to give up their weapons and obey the laws Mighty Joe proclaimed. Mighty Joe is not pleased with these individuals, and being now in the possession of all of our weapons, he begins to coerce these people to become subjects, like we are. According to Hobbes, these dissenters really have no basis for complaint, and certainly have no grounds for saying that Mighty Joe is unjust. After all, he made no agreement with them, and they made no agreement with anyone else. The dissenters are in that state of mistrust and suspicion that characterizes people who have not made any agreement with each other, and that means they just have to do the best they can to defend themselves. If someone comes along who is stronger than they are, too bad for them.

Mighty Joe is certainly in a very powerful position according to Hobbes. Since everyone has laid down their rights to him, he can walk around like a king, or a god. He can decide whether to raise an army; he can make any laws that he desires; he can decide what doctrines people can talk about; he can make decisions about what religions they can practice; he can decide rewards and punishments; he can determine who shall be honored. All the while he himself cannot be punished. What a life Mighty Joe will have.

Is a Sovereign That Bad?

At this point we may begin to wonder whether Hobbes was really serious. He seems to be advocating that the only way to have peace is for all of us to throw ourselves at the mercy of some Mighty Joe, on whom there would be no restrictions. His account of sovereignty seems to be foolish--we would never give up so much of our liberty, for it seems that we will wind up just being exploited by someone with tremendous power. In what way are we better off than if we had not made the agreement in the first place?

This seems to be an obvious objection to the view presented by Hobbes, but in fact, it is not fair to him. We have to remember that the sovereign is not necessarily one person. Furthermore, if we look at our own society, even with all of its checks and balances, Constitutional limitations on the power of the rulers, Bill of Rights, elected officials, etc., it is a very good example of just what Hobbes was talking about.

Even though Hobbes was a defender of monarchy (which we will see later), he was well aware that there were other possibilities for creating sovereignty than just giving it to one person. The sovereign is whoever is designated as having the ultimate power, and that can be an individual, a small group, or even a large group--the majority. If it is majority, that is where all of the power resides. It will be the majority who determines what the laws will be, what punishments will be given to those who break the laws, what wars will be fought, what taxes will be collected, what religions can be practiced and who shall be honored.

That is exactly what we have. The majority, by means of voting, determines all of these things. But, we might ask, what about the checks and balances and the other Constitutional limitations on the scope of government? The Constitution is just a document that derives its power from the fact that the majority has given it that power. Even in the Constitution itself, there is a process of amendment that can be used at any time. So if at some point, a big enough majority wants to change the Constitution, it will. If enough people want to scrap the Bill of Rights and institute a national religion, that is what will happen, whether it be Christianity, Islam, Hinduism, or old-time paganism. And even further, if the majority wants to throw out the Constitution completely and write a new document or just give all power to Mighty Joe, then that is what would happen.

That was Hobbes' main point. Once sovereignty has been established, there is no way to keep it in check. Hobbes did talk about some rights that people cannot lay down, like the right to self-preservation. A person can never just lay down his right to defend his own life, because Hobbes claimed that we only lay down our rights to gain something thereby. So if the sovereign goes wild, and begins to kill everyone, people will rebel and fight back. But the sovereign having so much power will be very difficult to overthrow. Sovereigns, once established, are very formidable monsters, but hopefully they will be useful ones.

The Complication Revisited

There is still a problem, however, in the establishment of the sovereign. Hobbes claimed that covenants made when there is no power to enforce them are void. That was the whole point in establishing a sovereign power. The question is how can the original contract be made, when at that point in time, there is no sovereign power to enforce it. The law of nature was that we should all lay down our rights if everyone else does too. Here we are on the island, each with our own weapon. I will give my weapon to Mighty Joe if all of the rest of you do too. But how do I know you will give up your weapons if there is no power right now, to enforce our agreement. Maybe we can all give them up at the same time. We will count, one, two, three, and on three, we will all throw them into the middle. Ready? One, two, two and one half, three. Can we all do this simultaneously? How can we make sure that others will throw in their weapons exactly when we do? It seems that we are going to have to trust others after all, but covenants made when there is no power to enforce the trust are invalid. Given the way that Hobbes set up the problem, is there any way that the sovereign power can be established? He tried to remove all trust, and just rely on fear of overwhelming power, but can this work? How can the sovereign power get off the ground?

Is Institution of Sovereignty by Fear the Solution?

Hobbes did say that there is another way that sovereigns can be established, and that is through fear. He also said that contracts and covenants made because of fear are valid. That means that if a mugger threatens us and says that we should give him our money and then he will spare our lives, this contract is a valid one. Hobbes thought that contracts made under duress are valid--that the reason that one agrees to the contract does not really matter. All that matters is that a person agreed to lay down a right.

The application of this view to the institution of the sovereign is straightforward. Suppose Mighty Joe invades our island and says that either we obey his laws or he will make us suffer. Mighty Joe is pretty strong and pretty terrifying, and he might even have an army of thugs to support him. In that case we will certainly have fear, and we will probably conclude that it would be better for us to just obey Mighty Joe's rules, and hope for the best.

This is apparently what Hobbes had in mind, but in this case, there are certainly strong objections to be raised against this view, for there is a good case to be made here that Hobbes was not being consistent. When a contract is made between Mighty Joe and us from fear, it seems that Mighty Joe is a party to the contract. But Hobbes specifically said before that the sovereign is not a party to the contract. Also, why would this contract be valid? Who is going to enforce it? Why would Mighty Joe have any reason to do anything for us? He says, your money or your life. We give him our money. Why should he then spare us our lives? There is obviously no power to make sure he keeps his part of the bargain, and Hobbes said before that contracts that cannot be enforced are void.

There does not seem to be any way to help Hobbes out on this point. Whether the sovereign is instituted by agreement or by fear, there is a definite problem about the establishment of the sovereign. Hobbes did not want to have the fundamental agreement based on trust. For him, trust can only occur once the sovereign has been set up. But there does not seem to be any way to do this that is consistent with the definitions of terms that Hobbes used. Fundamental trust has not been done away with. For society to be established, for the laws of nature to be fulfilled, and for us to live in peace, we will at some point have to trust.

Another Reason to Obey the Sovereign

While the argument for establishing the sovereign is not successful, there is another way that Hobbes made his case to convince us that we should submit to any existing sovereign. Let us put aside for the moment just how it was that the sovereign became established. The plain fact is that there are sovereigns aplenty around us, and the practical question for us is whether we should submit to what they dictate. Remember again, that the sovereign is not necessarily one person, but is a group, or even the majority. Is there some argument that can be given why we should go along with this great power, and not try to escape it?

Hobbes was personally very concerned with this question because of the chaos of the civil war that England and he had experienced. In his view civil war is the worst of all situations--it occurs when sovereignty breaks down and there is absolutely no trust. Civil wars are generally extremely brutal, and in the history of the United States, there were more American casualties in the four-year Civil War in the 1860's than the combined total of all of the other wars that America has fought in during its over two hundred years of existence.

This kind of point is the basis of Hobbes' argument. He admitted that submitting to a sovereign can be onerous, and since there are practically no limits on the sovereign's power, there is the definite possibility that the sovereign might exploit and even kill us. But consider the alternative, which according to Hobbes is civil war. Nothing could be worse than that, and so it is definitely worth it to throw in our lot with the sovereign. It is a much better bet for us to agree to obey him than it is try to make it on our own. The latter way is almost certain misery, and the former way at least gives us a chance. As Hobbes said the "the state of man can never be without some incommodity or other", and so we should at least try to give ourselves the best chance.

Furthermore, there are reasons to think that the sovereign might not take advantage of his great power over us. Sovereigns too, individuals or groups, are human beings, and so the same forces that work on us also work on them. One of these forces is the desire for a good reputation. The rulers of the past who have been corrupt and exploitative are now looked upon with scorn. Sovereigns know this, and they know that their reputation depends on the health of their subjects. This provides some restraint on them. And then there is also the ubiquitous fear of religion. There is always the unknown future, and the possibility that there is even a greater power that will punish people for their cruelties on the earth. This is also a constraint on sovereigns and is another reason why it would make sense to be obedient subjects.

This argument by Hobbes is an interesting one for a number of reasons. First, it is a practical, one might almost say a utilitarian argument. Hobbes was telling us to look at two situations and pick the one that has the best consequences. The choices are quite stark--either chaotic civil war, or possibly a peaceful situation. If these are the choices, it is quite clear what a reasonable person should do. The reasonable person should look at the alternatives, make a cost-benefit analysis, and choose the alternative that has the best consequences for themself.

One might assume that Hobbes was saying that this is the way that all people actually operate. But it is not necessary to attribute the view to Hobbes that all people are rational egoistic calculators. There is no doubt that many people are of this sort, and it is further undoubtedly true, that all of us have our moments (and plenty of them) when we do calculate in just this way. But whether this is a universal trait of people that they always follow is not a view that has to be attributed to Hobbes, and given his skepticism about other people, it would not be consistent with his main ideas to say that this is his view. Nevertheless, we can admit without much difficulty that arguments of this type will appeal to many, and will appeal to most of us a good deal of the time. For others, who operate under different motives, (in particular, religious people) Hobbes provided other arguments.

The other interesting point about the argument is Hobbes' attempt to reassure us that there will probably be some constraints on the sovereign. The constraints though will have to be appeals to the sovereign's self-interest. Again, it is not necessary to think that this is the only motive that people have. Maybe some sovereigns are very altruistic and have no greater desire than to make other people happy, and would gladly shed the burdens of rule except that they worry that no one could do a better job than they can. It is a wonderful thing if this kind of sovereign actually exists. But undoubtedly, there will be others who have coarser desires. Again, we cannot really know which sovereigns will be which, but even if they are of the lower variety, there will be constraints on them too. We have some reason to think that they will not go wild, but in the absence of any sovereign at all, there is no reason to be optimistic about our prospects.

The Classic Objection--Hobbes' Fool

Major thinkers are those who do not merely present their theories and views, but who also raise the strongest objections against their own ideas, and then have answers ready for these objections. Hobbes falls into the category of restless and honest thinkers who are not satisfied to just have a view, but also challenge it themselves to see if it can defended against the toughest criticisms.

The strongest objection Hobbes raised against his own view was in a section of *Leviathan* where he presented the problem of whether it is in line with reason to maintain our agreements after we have made them. Hobbes raised this objection in a colorful way, as he said that this is the way a fool might reason is his heart. Of course, calling the person who would do this kind of reasoning, a "fool", indicates that

Hobbes did not believe that the objection was insurmountable. Nevertheless, he permitted the fool to present a very strong case.

Here is what the fool says, or at least thinks in his heart. The fool wonders whether it is rational to keep to agreements, if one can gain a benefit by breaking them? Suppose that a sovereign has been instituted, and that laws have been put in place, and there is the awesome power that will punish anyone who does not keep their contract. No matter how awesome and terrifying the sovereign power is, it is still just a human being or a group of human beings. The sovereign is therefore not omniscient or omnipotent. So, if we are careful and disciplined, we might find situations where we can make a gain by breaking our contract. Of course, this will require very careful calculation and preparation, but such opportunities do arise in small and big ways.

First, consider some small ways. Once a sovereign has been established, there will very likely be a law against stealing. One of the most important functions of the sovereign, according to Hobbes, is to determine the rules of property and establish what is "mine" and "thine". Let us suppose that this has been done, and the fool has agreed to follow the laws of property, but he also finds himself in a supermarket and sees a very nice candy bar lying in a bin. Knowing that supermarkets do not just trust their customers, the fool checks around for mirrors, TV cameras and other workers in the store. The coast is clear. There is no way that he will be caught. In fact, the fool has actually done a little research and checked into the security system of the supermarket and he knows that he can get away with it. Why should he refrain? It is clearly in his interest to just steal the candy bar, for he can have it as his own and save the 50 cents that it would cost to buy it. Why would he be a fool for stealing it?

Here is an example of the fool thinking of violating his contract in a big way. The fool has devised a plan to take over the role of the sovereign himself. This will require assassination, and many other nasty acts. Again, this person may be called a fool, but he has planned it carefully. This is no action of a half-baked lunatic, but the plan of a disciplined and rigorous thinker, who has considered all of the risks and has prepared appropriate responses to them. He can get away with it-- there is very little doubt. If the plan is successful, and his careful calculations tell him it will be, he will be the sovereign, and wouldn't that be a great situation? He could then do anything, make any laws he wants, live in luxury, and have an army to defend himself against anyone who objects. The plan is set; it is foolproof. Why shouldn't he just do it?

Hobbes' fool raised the same question that Plato raised in the second book of the *Republic* in his story of Gyges' ring. Hobbes read Plato, and uncharacteristically, had many praise-worthy things to say about him, unlike Aristotle, about whom Hobbes never missed an opportunity to insult. In Plato's story, Gyges is a poor shepherd who finds a ring that he discovers makes him invisible, and thus gives him the powers of a god among men. Once Gyges realizes this, he uses the opportunity to kill the ruler of the city, seduce the queen, and make himself the tyrant. In the *Republic* Socrates is challenged to present an argument to Gyges why he should not use the great power that he has. Plato obviously thought that this problem was significant, because Socrates took up the next three hundred pages of the book developing his answer.

The Gyges story is a fantasy as is the idea of someone performing a successful coup d'etat against a sovereign in a modern state. Nevertheless, the problem raised by the fool and also by Gyges is a profound one that goes to the heart of Hobbes' solution to provide peace. Peace, according to Hobbes, is based on an agreement between people to follow certain institutions. People lay down their rights in order to get a better deal for themselves. It is reason, the laws of nature, which tell us to do this. But there is a problem that arises from the conception of reason that Hobbes used. In Hobbes' view reason tells us to do what is to our advantage. It tells us to weigh the consequences of the various alternatives that we have, and then do the one that is the best for us. This is a conception of reason that is based on enlightened self-interest. But what reason tells us, in this sense, may not coincide with what is considered "just", which Hobbes defined as keeping one's agreements. It is in our enlightened self-interest to avoid stealing if there is a chance of getting caught, and to avoid trying to kill the sovereign, if we face certain death. But if we look carefully, and if we are disciplined, we can find many Gyges-like situations where it will be in our self-interest to break agreements. The fool is asking this question--why should I keep an agreement that I made if I determine, and am quite certain, that I will gain by breaking the agreement? This is a very dangerous question, because it occurs to everyone, or to be more circumspect, to many people. If there are enough people convinced that the fool is right, the agreement to set up the sovereign will collapse, and we will be back into the condition of war. This is a critical problem.

Hobbes' Answer

Here are the reasons that Hobbes offered to refute the fool.

First, it is not rational to do something when it can turn out badly, and the risk involved cannot be calculated precisely. The fool cannot be that sure that he is in a Gyges-like situation. No matter how carefully he has planned, things do go awry, and so the risk the fool is taking is irrational.

Second, if the fool openly declares that he will break his contract with other people, he can never have confederates to help him with his plans. The only way that people will cooperate with him is if they are ignorant and foolish themselves, and no one can count on other people being that foolish.

Third, it is clearly mistaken to think that the fool will gain the joy of heaven by cheating on the contracts he made. The only way to get to heaven is by keeping one's contracts.

And fourth, even if the fool gains the position of the sovereign, which is very unlikely to begin with, by his act of rebelling he will be providing a role model for other would-be rebels. The fool's reign as sovereign will be fraught with rebels like himself.

Critique of Hobbes' Answer

These four reasons comprise Hobbes' answer, but do they really show that the fool is foolish? Actually, some of these points seem to be pretty foolish themselves. Consider the second reason. Would any reasonable fool declare that he is going to break his contract with other people? A person who would make such a declaration is truly a fool, and so this point of Hobbes just knocks down a fool made of straw. Anyone thinking of cheating, if they have any sense at all, will not tell other people about it. It is true, that there is a problem of having a group of cheaters cooperate with each other, for the reason that if there is no honor among thieves, then it is difficult for the thieves to complete their projects. This is an important point to consider, but it does not really deal with the most difficult problem, which is what kind of argument can one give to the solitary, disciplined, calculating cheater who does not boast, and cheats carefully and silently.

What about the first reason, that the fool can never be certain that he will get away with it. Of course, that is true, but on the other hand, nothing in life is certain and there is no guarantee that keeping one's contracts will provide advantages either. The question is whether there are situations where the risks of cheating are worth it, and this is an empirical matter that one can investigate, and the answer seems to be that there are such situations if one is looking for them. Many people cheat on their income taxes, some estimates are that 30% of Americans are income tax cheaters, and if one is prudent, the odds of getting caught are practically zero. Many people steal stamps and paper clips from the office. Many people shoplift and are successful. Of course, these are not of the magnitude of sovereign-cide, but they are violations of the basic agreement, and all of these actions do add up to something that has to be noted. Hobbes said that you will definitely get caught if you cheat. But the answer to him is probably not, if you are careful.

The third reason raises the old bugaboo of the righteous God who sees all and who will punish all misdeeds in the next life. It is odd, ironic and strange that Hobbes would use this as a reason not to cheat, especially because of what he says in a paragraph shortly following his statement of this reason. In this later paragraph Hobbes considered the kind of people who refuse to follow the established sovereign because they believe that they will be rewarded in heaven by God for their rebellion. Hobbes had very little patience with such types. He said that this is clearly irrational because no one knows what will happen after death. Beliefs in these matters are based on what other people have said, and they clearly do not know. But this very point would also tell against his third reason. How did Hobbes know whom God will reward or punish in the afterlife? Couldn't exactly the same point be raised on behalf of the fool? When Hobbes raised a point in one paragraph and then said almost the opposite two paragraphs later, it makes us wonder whether there he was thinking clearly and carefully, or whether he was including some hidden message. It certainly raises a question about the sincerity of the religious arguments that he used.

Finally, the fourth reason. Hobbes' argument here is probably sound, and a historical survey of successful rebels against a sovereign may indeed show that successful rebels are soon troubled by new rebels. But the problem with this answer is that there are all sorts of ways to break the contract besides trying to kill the sovereign and take over. The contract was one in which everyone agreed with each other to obey the laws the sovereign set down. Disobeying one of these laws is a violation of the basic contract. But if reason helps us to find the alternative that is best for us, Hobbes did not provide any good reason to convince us to keep the contract when violating it is clearly in our interest.

Modern Decision Theory--The Prisoner's Dilemma

The problem of the fool, and Hobbes' weak responses to it, present a difficulty that has perplexed and bothered political thinkers and others ever since Plato. The problem concerns the conception of reason that Hobbes was using. Hobbes and many others view reason as a capacity that does not provide us with goals to pursue, but just tells us the best way to accomplish the goals that we have. This is the instrumental view of reason. The fool's arguments point out a very disturbing problem about instrumental reason. While it would benefit every individual to live in a society in which everyone else is obedient to the laws of the sovereign, it would nevertheless benefit each individual even more to break the laws when they can get away with it. However, if each individual breaks the laws, the laws will collapse and everyone will lose the benefit of living in a law-abiding society. So while reason tells us to seek peace and to institute a sovereign so we can have a decent life, reason is also telling us to break our contracts when we can get away with it.

This particular problem has been examined by a new field of study called Decision Theory that has developed in the last few decades of the Twentieth Century. Decision theorists have spent a great deal of time and intellectual energy studying a problem called "the prisoner's dilemma" which reveals the fundamental problem that was raised by Hobbes' fool. Imagine two people who have been arrested for committing a robbery together. Each suspect is put into a separate room to be interrogated by the police. Neither of the suspects knows what the other suspect will say. While the two suspects did commit the robbery, the police do not really have enough evidence to convict either one of them for this crime. But the police do have enough evidence to convict these two individuals for some other crimes, but if both suspects keep quiet, neither one will have to serve the severe penalty for robbery. So without a confession from either one, each suspect will be in jail for one year. But if there is enough evidence developed to convict the suspects of robbery, they will have to serve a sentence of ten years.

The police then offer the following deal to one of the suspects. They say if you confess to the crime, you will go free, and the other person will serve the ten-year penalty. But they are also offering the same deal to the other suspect, and if he confesses and you do not, then he will go free and you will serve the severe penalty. But if you both confess, they cannot just turn you both free, but they will be somewhat lenient and have both of you serve a moderate penalty, three years.

In these conditions what should a particular suspect do? According to instrumental reason, he should think of the various alternatives and choose the one that is best for himself. So the suspect reasons, suppose the other confesses. Then if I don't, I will wind up being in jail for ten years, but if I also confess, I will only be in jail for three years. But let us suppose that the other keeps him mouth shut. Then if I confess, I go free, but if I keep my mouth shut too, I will still have to be in jail for one year. The conclusion is very clear. No matter what the other one does, I will be better off if I confess.

However, the other person is reasoning the same way, and he reasons that it is in his interest to confess too. So both suspects confess, and they both wind up serving three years. If they had trusted each other to keep quiet, they could have had only one year each, but reason told them to confess and they both wind up worse off.

The conclusion of a great many thinkers is that instrumental reason, the faculty that is supposed to enable us to achieve our goals, often gives us advice that makes us worse off. It does this in prisoner dilemma situations, which like the Gyges-situations are quite common. If we would all obey the rules, we would all prosper by living in a good society, but if everyone else obeys the rules and I don't, I get the benefit of living in a good society without paying the cost, and so I prosper even more. But everyone else can reason way too, and everyone will wind up disobeying the rules, being a fool in Hobbes' sense, and then we will all be worse off because our society will collapse or become corrupt. Each individual does what is best for himself, and as a result all individuals lose. That is the prisoner's dilemma and that is what happens when everyone thinks like the fool. But how can one prevent others from thinking in this way? Where is the mistake in this kind of reasoning? One might point out that when everyone thinks this way, disaster results, but the fool can reply, that is true, but my reasoning this way does not cause others to reason similarly. I do not tell others how to reason. Furthermore, if others actually already are cheating, I would be a real fool, to be obey the law, when it is about to collapse anyway.

What is evident from the prisoner's dilemma is that when both suspects follow instrumental reason, they do not get optimum results. Applying this to Hobbes, it means that if everyone reasons like the fool, we will all be in trouble. That may be true, but that is not enough to point out that there is a mistake in any particular fool's reasoning.

Reason is Weak--Peace Requires the Passions

The failure of the arguments against the fool, and also the modern example of the prisoner's dilemma point to a real problem of trying to establish cooperation and obedience to the law on the basis of the conception of instrumental reason. If one thinks of reason as determining which alternative will be the best for us, then there is a serious problem, for what is best for each individual turns out to be terrible for us as a group. Yet, we can only make our own decisions about what to do as individuals.

This leads to us wondering about instrumental reason itself. Perhaps this faculty is not the great proponent of peace as Hobbes originally claimed. Reason also seems to be a villain, whispering in our ear to break the law, that it is in our interest to do so, and that we will better off thereby no matter what other people are doing.

But Hobbes was aware of this point too. He did not have great faith in reason as the way to provide peace. At best he said that reason could suggest a solution, the sovereign, but reason, by itself, would not be enough to move us in that direction. This skepticism about the power of reason on Hobbes' part may be due in part because he thought that reason is too weak to withstand the pressure of the passions that lead us to war. But it could also be that reason does not just tell us to be quiet and cooperative; it also insinuates that it would be a good idea to break our contracts. If we are going to have peace, there had better be other capacities besides reason that will push us in the right direction.

Fortunately, Hobbes said, there are other factors that push us toward peace. In particular the passion of fear is very helpful in this regard. The sovereign provides the force and terror that will frighten us into keeping our word. Our fear of death and wounds will keep us honest. However, we have seen that there are significant problems in establishing a sovereign when fear and suspicion are the primary motivators.

It could very well be that Hobbes was right in general, about the necessity of the passions as motivators for getting us to be peaceful, but when he emphasized the negative passions it was to the detriment of his theory. Hobbes wanted to establish trust in a non-circular way, but there may be no way to do this, and trust itself could very well be one of the primary motivators of people that leads to cooperation and peace. We may not be able to read other people well enough to tell if they are trustworthy or not, and many turn out not to be, but still, we do have basic trust in others, at least enough to establish some authority and some laws. Trust of this basic sort is also a passion, and it can be strong enough to overcome the selfish designs of instrumental reason. Hobbes was trying to establish some other factor as a basis for trust, but it does not appear that he was successful. At bottom, it might be that trust is what gets the whole thing going

Different Kinds of Sovereigns--Why Monarchy is Best

While there is no question that Hobbes thought that there could be sovereigns of different types, when he talked about the sovereign, he was thinking of a monarch, and he left no doubt in anyone's mind that he thought that monarchy was the best form of government. This was a critical issue for Hobbes because he lived through the English Revolution when Cromwell overthrew the English king, who was later restored. Throughout these changes Hobbes was always on the side of the monarchy, and at one point he boasted that he was the first to flee England when the monarchy was under attack in the early stages of the Revolution.

According to Hobbes there are basically three types of sovereignty--monarchy, aristocracy and democracy. The distinction between them is clear--how many individuals make up the sovereign. In monarchy it is one person, in aristocracy it is a few people, and in democracy sovereignty is basically open to anyone. All other forms of sovereignty can be reduced to these three models. For example, an elected king is really a form of democracy, because the people still maintain the ultimate power.

When Hobbes looked at the different forms that sovereignty could assume, he was quite convinced that monarchy was the best. But he did not defend it in religious terms, as the divine right of kings, but rather on the very pragmatic grounds that it would be the most likely to provide peace and security.   Hobbes provided a number of reasons to support his view. First, while a monarch is supposed to provide for the public benefits of peace and security, the monarch is still an individual with his or her own personal desires and goals. Like all people, the monarch will want fame, a good reputation, and riches for his friends and family.   But a monarch's reputation and resources are very dependent on the health of the community over which he reigns. So there is actually an overlap between private and public interest. However, in forms of government where the sovereignty is divided among a few or even a great number of people, there is no such overlap. If an individual representative in a democracy is corrupt, it does not follow that the public as a whole will suffer that much and so the reputation of the individual representative is not as closely tied to the welfare of the general community. For this reason, each representative has a greater interest to cheat and be corrupt than does the individual monarch. So, Hobbes reasoned, there will probably be more corruption in non-monarchical forms of government.

There is another reason to expect that monarchies will be more efficient. One reason that people fight is because there is equality between them, and there is no overwhelming power to keep them to their agreements. Hobbes called this kind of situation the state of nature, and we institute a sovereign to escape it. In an aristocracy or a democracy, the group of people who are the rulers will be, in effect, in a state of nature with respect to each other. There is no one overpowering force looming over them to punish them if they break their agreements. Instead, they all have equal power, and this means that they will be suspicious, will be competing for honor and glory, and will have no reason to trust that others will be peaceful and reliable. The conditions of war will exist for the group of rulers, relative to each other. Hobbes expected that democratic assemblies and even councils of aristocrats, would be full of rivalry, antagonism, treachery and conflict. On the other hand, monarchy does not have this problem. There are no people equal to the king or queen; everyone is below them. There is a much better chance that this kind of sovereign will perform the duty of keeping the peace.

There are special problems too with monarchies, but Hobbes said that no human institution is without inconveniences. The trick is to arrange things to reduce the inconvenience as much as possible. The main problem of monarchies is the succession issue, but this can be handled, and the best way is to let the current monarch choose who the successor will be. There is also the possibility that the monarch will be an infant, or someone without the capacity to perform the duties of the office. Hobbes admitted that these are certainly problems and difficulties, but what we have to do is to compare these problems with our other alternatives: aristocracy and democracy, which he thought were more likely to lead to civil war. Those other conditions are even worse, and so to change a statement that Winston Churchill made about democracy, monarchy is a form of government with many problems, and its only saving grace is that it is still better than all of the others.

Assessment of Hobbes' Argument Concerning Monarchy

Hobbes presented some provocative arguments concerning the superiority of monarchy, and it is interesting to consider why these arguments are no longer acceptable. What do we now know that he did not? One point is that in the 20th Century we have experience with quasi-monarchical rulers like Hitler, Stalin, Pol Pot, Saddam Hussein, and unfortunately many others. These individuals certainly make one wonder about Hobbes' claim that as bad as a monarch might be, he certainly would be better than the situation in which there is no sovereign at all. Given characters like Hitler and his ilk, that just does not seem to be true. It could be that Twentieth Century technology has given dictators and tyrants the kind of power for exploitation that Hobbes could not possibly have imagined, and for that reason his arguments no longer apply to us.

But Hobbes' arguments against aristocracy and democracy are also problematic. He over-estimated the turbulence and insecurity that would ensue when sovereignty is divided among a number of people, all of whom are in an equal position relative to each other. As we have seen, for Hobbes, the individuals in whom sovereignty resides will be in a state of nature with respect to each other, and given his view, this means they must be suspicious, envious, and hostile, just to protect themselves. But that is not the case in practice, for it turns out that representative democracies have been among the more stable forms of government, and that monarchies and dictatorships, in the Twentieth Century at least, do not last very long. Answering this question can point to some revealing weaknesses in the whole theory that Hobbes constructed.

One reason to explain why Hobbes' views about democracies are incorrect is that he misunderstood the relation between the sovereign and the people. In Hobbes' view, there is no agreement between the sovereign and the subjects; rather, the people make an agreement with each other to obey the sovereign, but there is nothing binding the sovereign to any agreement. That means that the people elected in a democracy to make and enforce the rules have not made an agreement with the subjects or with each other. For Hobbes that meant that there would be no restraint on conflicts between them.

As a matter of fact, however, it does not work that way. First of all, the elected officials in a democracy do have a kind of agreement with the people who elected them, and it is an agreement that they adhere to. The agreement is that the officials can hold office and have power as long as they keep being elected, but once they are voted out of office, they have to give up the power that they held. Hobbes would consider it very odd that people who have enormous power just give it up at certain points and let other people take it. Why doesn't someone who commands an army just throw the newly elected official in jail instead of simply relinquishing the power and retiring to private life?

And yet this is exactly what happens. For Hobbes it is exceedingly strange, and when one accepts his views about human nature and the characteristics of sovereignty it does seem strange, for it means that people make agreements and keep to them even when they are not subject to awesome threats. In the United States the President agrees to follow the Constitution, a document written over two hundred years ago. Once in office, the President could easily violate the Constitution, and do all sorts of terrible things, and use his power to prevent the Congress from impeaching him. And yet this does not happen. It seems to be the case that just the effect of agreeing to obey this old document is enough to keep these admittedly ambitious, vain-glorious people in line. Hobbes would have predicted that it would never work. But it has, and that means that Hobbes' views about how agreements work between people are faulty. Sometimes, at least, just making an agreement, by itself, is sufficient for having most people follow it, even if many of the people know that the agreement will not be enforced by threats of punishment.

Also, Parliaments and Congresses do not inevitably dissolve into civil wars as Hobbes would have also predicted. Hobbes thought if there was no over-arching force, and if people were in a position of equality relative to each other, they would soon be fighting without restraint, and yet, the general experience is that representatives do restrain themselves. They restrain themselves because they agree to, even though there might not be a power to enforce this agreement. This is another instance of the same point--people will generally keep an agreement just because they made one, even though there is no way to enforce it. This does not mean that everyone will keep the agreement. There will be cheaters, but even if we cannot tell who the cheaters are, most of us will stick to what we said we would do. So there must be some flaw in Hobbes' account of how people think and act.

4

Religion

But maybe there is an answer that Hobbes could supply to the criticism of his views mentioned at the end of the last chapter--an answer that is very much in line with the general train of his thought. This answer is that what binds people to agreements when there is no civil sovereign, is their fear of the REALLY BIG SOVEREIGN, the Supernatural One, who knows everything that we do and will not look kindly on anyone who breaks their contracts.

There are certainly passages where Hobbes did present a view of this sort, and he also suggested that fear of God's wrath might keep the human sovereigns in line too. Hobbes was aware that religion could be very useful in keeping peace in the community, but he was also aware that it could be a divisive force. Many of the strains that led to the civil war in England had a sectarian basis, and Hobbes realized that people who take religion seriously tend to not be very understanding of those who have different views. For that reason Hobbes claimed that the sovereign has the right to set the parameters for religious observation and belief, and that whatever religion the sovereign chooses should be the one that subjects should obey.

In some ways this is a cynical view of religion that raises the issue of whether Hobbes himself was religious and believed in God. This is not only an interesting question for us, but it also concerned his contemporaries, for a frequent accusation that was made by those who disagreed with him was that Hobbes was an atheist. Hobbes, himself, declared that he was not, but there is reason to believe that he was not telling the truth. It was definitely not prudent to claim to be an atheist, when there were believers ready to light bonfires, and Hobbes claimed that he was a prudent man. But no matter what Hobbes actually professed, many thought him to actually be an atheist, and he lived under a cloud of suspicion for many years. It was only the protection of powerful patrons that kept him out of serious trouble.

There are three main issues about Hobbes' views about religion that are worth examining. The first is, what role did Hobbes assign to religion in his political philosophy. Did Hobbes think that religion actually did play some essential role in the establishment and the maintenance of civil society? But also, what was Hobbes' own view of religion? Even if he thought that religious belief had useful aspects, did he have such beliefs himself? Finally, a good part of Hobbes's major work, *Leviathan*, is devoted to the discussion of the Christian commonwealth. Does this big section of *Leviathan* show that Hobbes thought that religion was essential for a society and that he believed in it himself?

Is Religion Essential?

Hobbes was always very interested in religion and its role in society. He was well aware of the trouble that religion could cause, but he also realized that it could be very useful. The question is whether ultimately, Hobbes thought that it is the fear of God, and not the fear of any sovereign that humans create, that is necessary to underwrite the agreements that lead to the development of peace.

There are some suggestions that Hobbes did have this view. After all, he said that one thing we can know about other people is that fear is a predominant emotion, and the evidence for that is the universality of religion. Also, one of Hobbes' answers to the fool specifically mentioned the fear of after-life punishments as a reason to keep one's contracts.

These points, and others that Hobbes made, show that he did think that religious belief had its uses, but they do not show that he believed that religious belief and the fear that it engendered were the ultimate bases of peace. The whole aim of Hobbes's view was to provide a minimalist account of war and especially of peace--an account that would appeal to anyone who was rational, and was not necessarily designed to appeal to any particular religious group or to religious people in general. If Hobbes' argument was to be successful in his own eyes, it should convince everyone--the religious and the atheists.

Still, there is a question to be raised. While Hobbes may have desired and even preferred that an appeal to religious fear be unnecessary, perhaps there is no way to avoid it given the way he set up the problem of cooperation? What could prevent Gyges from taking advantage besides his thinking that an all-seeing God would note his crimes and would exact punishment in the next world? According to Hobbes there will only be cooperation and peace when there is an over-powering and awesome force to ensure that people will keep their word, and clearly, no human sovereign could provide the necessary command and control. We, who live in the Age of Technology, are aware of totalitarian capacities that would have amazed Hobbes, and we know how the state can be a Leviathan in ways Hobbes could only dream about. But still even Hitler and Stalin, with all of their ruthlessness, paranoia, armies of informers, and sophisticated spying equipment, still had rebels and dissidents to deal with. Human sovereigns seem to be incapable of doing what is necessary to establish complete compliance with the law and perhaps only belief in God will provide the requisite fear and sanctions.

This is an interesting twist to Hobbes' general view of the situation, but he would not have to agree with it. Hobbes' theory does not actually require an all-powerful Big Bopper Sovereign to work. Hobbes was well aware that no sovereign made of humans would be all-powerful, and that meant that there would always be those who would rebel and break the law. But the question is how many rebels would there be? A peaceful society can tolerate a few law-breakers-- we have the police to take care of them. A peaceful society can even tolerate a few law-breakers who get away with it. The question is whether the number of such successful law-breakers can be kept under the threshold that causes a breakdown of the society. The sovereign might be powerful enough, and often is, to keep the number of law-breakers under the critical threshold. If everyone were to look at the situation like the fool--rationally calculate one's chances of getting away with cheating--the system might collapse. But fortunately, there are not that many fools. Many people are not ready to take any risks, and many others don't bother to make such calculations and take the easy path of just obeying the law. Many are also frightened by threats of terrible punishments, even if it would be rational to take the chance, because the pay-off of success would be so great. So to support Hobbes' view, the institution of a human sovereign could very well be sufficient to shift the balance of forces enough so that most people will be intimidated into keeping their word, and that would enable peace and cooperation to develop and flourish.

There is, however, a problem with the above Hobbsian response. He said that we cannot "read" other people, and so while most people may be cowed into obedience by the sovereign, we can never be sure which people are the rebellious ones. That means we would have to be suspicious of everyone, and again consider making pre-emptive strikes, and soon there would be the war of all against all. Even if we know that 99% of the population is obedient, since we cannot identify the recalcitrant 1%, we had better suspect everyone. So if we cannot be confident of everyone, we cannot be confident of anyone.

This is definitely a problem for Hobbes, because once one has let the skeptical genie out of the bottle, it can raise all kinds of havoc, and may not permit the development of peace. However, making God the ultimate sovereign will not solve this particular problem. For not even promoting belief in a sovereign God can assure us that 100% will keep their word. In spite of universal religious belief, we can be sure that there will still be some cheaters.

So while a human sovereign cannot command universal compliance, neither can belief in an omnipotent God. There will probably always be law-breakers. Nevertheless, there is some actual threshold that we use to tolerate criminals in our midst. We know that there are some criminals out there now, and we cannot always identify them, but still, we are not suspicious of everyone.

One final point. Is God Hobbes' ace in the hole to keep the sovereign in line? Given his view that the sovereign is not part of the agreement to keep peace, what restraint is there on him? Maybe it would be a very useful idea to try to develop religious belief in the sovereign, so he will be afraid that God will punish any contemplated corruption.

But Hobbes did not think this was the only possible way to restrain a wild sovereign. There are also the factors of self-interest and vain-glory. No one wants to be known or remembered as being a cruel and awful tyrant. Even the actual cruel and awful tyrants try as best as they can to have history written in their favor. They know that sovereigns are judged in terms of the health and welfare of their subjects, and knowing this may be enough to keep sovereigns from excessively exploiting their position too much. Thus, a belief in a righteous God who will punish the wicked would be useful to instill in the sovereign, but it is not necessary.

Was Hobbes an Atheist?

Hobbes thought that religious belief could be useful both for the sovereign and the subjects, but did he think that it was just a useful fiction? Was Hobbes down deep an atheist?

Of course, if he were, he would never have admitted it. Even in our liberal and tolerant times, many people feel uneasy about professing to be non-believers, probably because they are in such a small minority. But in Hobbes' day, it was not just that the open atheist might get a few hard stares, and maybe even a threatening letter or two. At that time there were very serious reactions to heresy, let alone atheism. Hobbes, being a self-confessed cautious type, would never have put himself in such a vulnerable position.

And yet, for all of his professions of belief, many of Hobbes' contemporaries did accuse him of being an atheist, and not just for the reason that they were just looking for some bad name to call him because they did not like him for other reasons. There are many passages in Hobbes' writings that make one wonder. Here are three points that Hobbes made that can be seen as indicating that he also applied his skepticism to religious matters.

First, there is his definition of religion--that it is a type of fear. While he did say that true religion occurs when the cause of the fear actually exists, he did not say that any religion is actually true. His definitions were hypothetical--this is what it would be for a religion to be true. This kind of definition does not show that Hobbes was a non-believer, but it is odd that he did not take the opportunity to say that any religious view is true.

A second point is that Hobbes clearly stated that peoples' religious practices and professions should follow whatever religion the sovereign proclaims to be the official one. He followed this practice scrupulously himself. Again this does not show that Hobbes was an atheist, but it is difficult to square this view with someone who has a sincere belief in a particular religion. It would also follow that if the sovereign proclaimed that there would be no religious practices, something Hobbes probably would have trouble imagining, then on Hobbes view that is what should be also followed. Is this the kind of view that would be put forward by a sincere believer?

One final interesting piece of evidence on this question concerns the way Hobbes used the Bible to show that his doctrines were consistent with Scripture. Hobbes quoted the following passage from Samuel I, chapter 8, verses 11, 12, etc.

This shall be the right of the king you will have to reign over you. He shall take your sons, and set them to drive his chariots, and to be his horsemen, and to run before his chariots; and gather in his harvest; and to make his engines of war, and instruments of his chariots; and shall take your daughters to make perfumes, to be his cooks, and bakers. He shall take your fields, your vineyards, and your olive-yards, and give them to his servants. He shall take the tithe of your corn and wine, and give it to the men of his chamber, and to his other servants. He shall take your man-servants and your maid-servants, and the choice of your youth, and employ them in his business. He shall take the tithe of your flocks; and you shall be his servants.

Hobbes used this passage to show that the Bible agreed with his view that there is no constraint on the sovereign's power and that he has the right to do anything since he made no agreement to limit himself. This is an amusing interpretation of the passage, because the context makes it quite clear that the point of this passage, which is stated by the prophet Samuel, is to discourage the people of Israel from having a king. The people were clamoring for a king so that they could be like other nations, and Samuel says, in effect, "Why do you want one? A king will only exploit you and make you miserable." Hobbes used this passage to say, "See, the Bible itself says that there is no limit on the sovereign's power." The cynical point of Hobbes' interpretation is that he undoubtedly knew quite well that Samuel was disapproving of the way that kings act, and yet, Hobbes used the passage to claim that the Bible is in accord with his own views. It is unlikely that a person who took the Bible seriously would twist it in this way.

These are just three points of many that could be picked out of Hobbes' writings that indicate that he probably was not a very orthodox believer, or at least he did not follow any of the standard Christian views that were around in his time. When one combines this attitude with his very sincere belief in materialism, and his arguments that an immaterial substance is a contradiction in terms, one can see why many of his contemporaries thought that he was an atheist. They were probably right.

Why is So Much of Leviathan Devoted to Christianity?

Still there are other questions to raise if we conclude that Hobbes was an atheist. If we look at *Leviathan*, his most complete and developed philosophical work, we will see that almost half of it is devoted to a discussion of what a Christian commonwealth would be, and in this part he also discussed many questions of Christian doctrine and theology. Why would an atheist write that much about such topics?

The answer to the above question is quite clear. Hobbes knew that the audience for his book would consist mainly of Christians. He also thought that the acceptance of his views was critical for the establishment and maintenance of peace. Therefore, it was very important to show that his doctrines and ideas were consistent with Christian doctrine and also had Scriptural support. In particular, Hobbes thought that it was very important that everyone accept his view that in religious matters, everyone should obey the dictates of the sovereign. How exactly could this be given a Scriptural basis and be made consistent with Christian doctrine, especially, when as was so evident to Hobbes, Christians widely diverged on what they believed God was saying to them?

Hobbes' Interpretations of the Bible

Prophesy--The views that Hobbes presented are an interesting mixture of skepticism about religion, professions of piety and skillful use of the Biblical quotations. The conclusion reached is that the Bible is fully in accord with Hobbes' views about the powers of the sovereign, even in the establishment of religion. It is really quite a virtuoso performance, even if it does not seem to have convinced anyone.

Hobbes began his argument with a skeptical shot across the bow. He asked, is it possible for us to determine if someone who claims that God spoke to him is really telling the truth. He admitted that if God did speak to someone, the person would know it very well, but the problem is how do we, the observers, determine who is a true prophet and who is a charlatan. This is no idle question, for we know that there are a great number of charlatans out there, because there are so many people claiming that God spoke to them, but they report God saying different things, often inconsistent with each other. Even worse, these various claims about God's words, are the cause of conflict and war--a severe problem in Hobbes' time as in our own.

Hobbes used the Bible to show that there are two criteria to determine who is a true prophet. First, the alleged prophet must be able to perform miracles, and then the prophet's statements have to be consistent with God's doctrines. The matter of miracles is of little value to us anymore as a criterion, because for one reason or another miracles no longer seem to occur. So the whole matter rests on what the alleged prophets say--their statements can only come from God if they are consistent with God's doctrines. But how do we determine what is consistent with God's doctrines? We have two sources--one is the laws of nature, which God has given us the capacity of reason to determine, and the other is statements in the Bible itself. The laws of nature are those propositions that reason tells us we must follow to have peace, and that Hobbes already revealed. So, if an alleged prophet said anything that conflicted with what Hobbes told us is necessary for peace, then the alleged prophet shows himself to be a fraud. And what happens when we look in the Bible? Once again, Hobbes used his interpretative legerdemain to show that the Bible itself agrees with Hobbsian views about the powers of the sovereign. The conclusion is that someone shows himself to be a charlatan if they say that God told them something that conflicts with the doctrines of Hobbes.

This is quite a breath-taking conclusion. Hobbes said that there is Biblical support for the view that everyone should obey the dictates of the sovereign on religion, no matter what those dictates are, and anyone who says differently is a false prophet.

Miracles--Hobbes was also very skeptical about miracles. His argument is very similar in structure to the argument about prophecy. The beginning point is a skeptical one. As an observer there is no way to tell whether what one is witnessing is a true miracle or just a trick. There is Biblical authority to support this point, Hobbes claimed. When Moses came to see the Pharoah, he performed various miracles to provide his bona fides as a true prophet. But the Egyptian magicians did the same things. Now we know, said Hobbes, that what Moses did was actually a miracle and that the Egyptians were just tricksters, but on the face of it, they were doing the same thing, and so the question is how to distinguish the difference.

The only way is by seeing what doctrine the exhibition of miracles is supposed to lead to. Say that we see someone do something marvelous and strange that seems to violate the usual laws of physics. But if this demonstration is designed to encourage belief in some doctrine that is inconsistent with the proper views, then it is no miracle, but is a fraud. Just as in the case of prophesy, the ultimate test is the view that is being propagated. And what are the proper views? The answer again is that they are the views consistent with Hobbes' doctrines. Of course, he did not put it that way, but that is exactly what it amounts to.

This has one very interesting consequence. According to Hobbes the sovereign is the authority that decides matters of religious practice and observance. Since one cannot tell just by looking whether a miracle has occurred, and since it might be an important matter, it is the sovereign's role to make the judgment. If the sovereign says that a miracle has really occurred, then it has. And if not, not. This is another instance of matters of religious authenticity being decided by a civil authority.

Religion and Materialism--Hobbes was a militant materialist as he thought that the concept of an immaterial body was an absurdity in the same way as is a round square. But Hobbes also thought that it was important to show that his view was fully consistent with Scriptures and that he was not saying anything in violation of Christianity by holding this view. On the face of it, this would be a difficult position to hold, but Hobbes managed it, again by some interesting arguments and by some fanciful interpretations of Biblical passages.

There were two problems in making the case that the Bible is consistent with materialism. The first is the nature of God and the second is the character of the angels and spirits that are referred to in the Bible. Concerning the nature of God, Hobbes relied on the view that we can know nothing about God's qualities. We only know *that* he is, but we can never know *what* he is. So, Hobbes inferred, we cannot say that he is not material. Hobbes was relying on the tricky maneuver of the double negative to keep open the possibility that God might be material. In any case, we cannot rule it out.

Concerning the angels and spirits, Hobbes claimed that there is nothing in the Bible that would be inconsistent with saying that they are material bodies, but of a gossamer kind. The Bible also says that some people are spiritually moved to act in a certain way. What this means, Hobbes said, is that their movement was caused by some mental force. For Hobbes, a mental force is a phantasm of some sort, and he already told us in the very beginning of *Leviathan* that phantasms are material.

The Afterlife--Hobbes extended his relentless materialism even to his view of the afterlife. First, let us consider heaven. It is not some mystical place where non-corporeal beings commune, but rather, heaven is this very earth and eternal life for those who will receive it, is a completely physical life with our resurrected bodies. Again, Hobbes said this is not just his peculiar view of the matter, but one can find it in the Bible itself, if one will just consider the relevant passages and interpret them in the correct way.

What about hell and its eternal torments? Where is hell located and do the torments actually occur? On this point Hobbes said that we have to take a metaphorical view of what the Bible is saying. Sinners will be punished, all right, but not by burning in sulphurous flames. Rather, the punishment is that they do not get the opportunity to be resurrected, and so they will just be dead. Since life is what everyone wants most of all, and fear of death is the worst fear, the sinners are deprived of what they would have most wanted. Sinners are merely mortal, but the good get to have eternal life.

Did Hobbes Really Believe This?

If Hobbes was an atheist, why did he insist on presenting these non-standard interpretations of the Bible? Why did he insist on saying that the Bible was consistent with materialism, when it was generally believed that materialism implied atheism?

Part of the explanation is that Hobbes wanted to show that no matter how apparently anti-religious his views were, that they were consistent with what the Bible actually did say. Again, Hobbes knew his audience very well, and he knew that his views would not be accepted if they were understood as being in deep conflict with the Scriptures. So there was certainly a point to his attempt to show that when properly read, the Bible itself was in accord with materialism and all of its consequences.

But there is another aspect of all of this that is strange and puzzling, and that concerns Hobbes' character. On the one hand he liked to portray himself as a very cautious person, one who carefully weighed the pro's and con's before doing anything, and who was prudence personified. And yet, in his comments on and quotations from the Bible, he seemed to be going out of his way to thumb his nose at the traditional views and interpretations. He claimed that the Bible itself is in accord with his own views, even when he knew they would be taken at the very least to be skirting the edges of atheism. This ambivalence on Hobbes' part was a long-apparent feature of his character. On the one hand, he counseled prudence and caution, but on the other, he was himself bold and audacious and seemed to delight in attacking powerful religious authorities that could, and did, make trouble for him.

The Civil Authority Takes Precedence Over the Religious Authority

The most significant practical point of Hobbes' interpretation of the Bible was his claim that the civil authority always takes precedence over the religious authority in a commonwealth. This was one of the major disputes of Hobbes' time, and he came down squarely on the secular side, with hardly any qualification. The sovereign in Hobbes' view has the right to determine religious practice and what doctrines can be taught, and as we have seen, to determine who are the true prophets and what are the true miracles.

Christ is the King, Hobbes admitted, but as the Bible says, the King of the world to come. When the good are resurrected, then Christ will be the one to rule and to obey. But until that day, it is the civil authority that takes precedence. Furthermore, this is what the Bible itself says.

But what if the sovereign is not a Christian? What if the sovereign is even hostile to Christianity and insists that the subjects disavow it publicly? Even so, Hobbes said, the subjects should obey the sovereign and do the acts that are required. Of course, the sovereign only controls public actions and cannot control private thoughts, and so people can believe anything they want to, and profess the utmost piety in their own minds. But the sovereign is in control of all public expressions of belief and faith, and if the sovereign demands that people publicly reject Christianity, then that is what subjects should do. All of this follows from Hobbes' political arguments, but if these are not acceptable, or if the arguments are too complex to be followed, then Hobbes also demonstrated how one can also find his view expressed in the Bible.

Hobbes, the First Secular Humanist

In spite of all the discussion of religion by Hobbes, and in spite of his great interest in it, it is clear that he was interested in down-playing the importance of religion, and that he wanted to establish the basis of government and authority just on secular grounds. Religion was of interest to Hobbes because of the effects that religious belief has on people. Whether those beliefs happen to be true was of much less importance. What really mattered to Hobbes was that life be peaceful, that people not kill each other, and that they have the chance to fulfill their individual and social aims. Oh yes, he did discuss the afterlife and heaven, but even there, the afterlife is curiously much like current life, only there is no death. Hobbes realized that he had to show that his views were consistent with Christianity if he was to get any hearing at all, as well as avoid the stake, but the whole emphasis in his work is against taking the theological doctrines of religion and their implications seriously. In spite of all of his protestations, it seems likely that Hobbes himself did not hold orthodox Christian views in his heart. In any case theology for Hobbes concerned what people say privately to themselves. It did not play an important role in ordering life, making peace, or fulfilling desires.

5

Aspects of Materialism

Two Controversies

Hobbes was an adamant materialist, and since he was also a rigorous and systematic thinker, he was interested in seeing what followed from materialism. Also, he was not the kind of person who would avoid a controversial implication of his views. He was quite aware that his ideas would provoke responses from the leading religious and secular thinkers, but as we saw above, there was an aspect of Hobbes that relished a good fight. Among the controversies that he engaged in during his long life, two will be examined below. The first concerned his dispute with Bishop Bramhall about free will and the second is the discussion he had with the Rene Descartes concerning the short book, *Meditations*, that Descartes had written. Both controversies centered on the issue of materialism.

Free Will

Hobbes was quite clear about the notion of free will. There was no such thing. Since everything was just matter in motion, and since nothing could move itself, all motions were caused by something else that was moving. Thus the idea that anything could have the free will to move itself made no sense.

Furthermore, he thought that the concept of free will was confused. Suppose that after a period of deliberation, I decide to leave my house and go for a walk. If there is nothing that is preventing me from doing this, then my will is free, or in Hobbes' terms, I have liberty. Suppose that after deliberating, I decide to stay in the house, and nothing compels me to leave. In that case I am free too. But the defenders of free will say that more is involved than just that. They claim that when one has free will, nothing is preventing or compelling the decision itself. In Hobbes' terms, that means I can will what I will. This, Hobbes says, makes no sense, for it leads to an infinite regress. It would also mean that I can will what I will what I will, and so on. Free will in this latter sense just collapses into nonsense.

What happens when we make a decision according to Hobbes? There is simply a power struggle of various passions within us, some pulling us in one direction, and some in another. If this struggle does get resolved, then ultimately, the forces of one side will win out, and these forces will have the "last say" and will cause the action that we take. The winning side is our decision, or our will, and is the last thing that occurs in our minds before the action itself. The struggle itself is a conflict of motions and is subject to the general law that everything that moves is moved by something else. There is nothing in the struggle that could be characterized as moving itself. Yet, we do have liberty if the winning side in the struggle gets to carry out the action that it has designated. So our actions are subject to the laws of motion, which Hobbes calls necessary, and yet, we also have liberty. There is no conflict between necessity and liberty. There only seems to be a conflict to those who do not understand what these terms mean. If we asked Hobbes if there is a long chain of causes that leads to our actions, and that causes them to happen, he would have said yes, that is correct. And if we asked him if we have then also have liberty, he would reply, sometimes, if nothing prevents us from acting according to our decision.

Bishop Bramhall was outraged by Hobbes' view. The Bishop thought that it conflicted with Christian doctrine, with the statements of the Bible and with morality and with common sense. The record of his dispute with Hobbes is long, and actually quite tedious. Both disputants play the game of Scriptural quotation, but this is of little concern to us, although it is amusing to see Hobbes quote and twist the Bible to support his own views. But Bramhall does raise some interesting questions. In particular, Bramhall was concerned with the question of how Hobbes' view squares with our understanding of morality and justice. If Hobbes' view is correct, then there is a cause for all of our actions, and as Hobbes said himself, they are all necessitated. This means that our actions could not be different than they are. But if that is so, how can we praise or blame people for what they do? When we praise someone for knocking down the bank robber and thus enabling the police to catch him, we assume this person's heroic action was up to him. We blame the bank robber because we assume this criminal thought about and planned his crime, and then as a result of this deliberation, carried it out. But if the actions of both parties are necessitated, then the praise and blame is misplaced. We wouldn't praise the hero, if he just happened to be in the right spot on the sidewalk, and the bank robber unwittingly tripped over the hero's foot. We wouldn't condemn the bank robber, if he didn't really plan the crime, but was just the hypnotized agent of some master-thug. In other words, praising and blaming people has to be based on the assumption that people have free will.

Furthermore, our whole conception of justice also depends on the assumption that people have free will, at least some of the time. If the bank robber is caught and sent to prison, this would be unjust if the robber was not in control of his actions. If everything is necessitated, as Hobbes said, how can we justly punish anyone? What would be the point of having laws, for they would all be unjust, and they would not be able to affect peoples' deliberations about what to do anyway. On the necessity view, everything we do was determined a long time ago.

Hobbes' reply was that Bramhall's objections betray a very serious misunderstanding of the meanings of certain terms, in particular 'will' and 'liberty'. Once these terms are correctly understood, it will become apparent that there is no conflict between the view that all of our actions are necessitated, and that it is just to punish criminals, to praise heroes and to condemn villains. As far as justice goes, it is just to punish someone if they commit a misdeed voluntarily. People act voluntarily when they act according to their will, and their will is simply the last in the long line of causes that occurs within them. 'Justice' means nothing more than that, and it is clear that many punishments are therefore just. Furthermore, laws are just because they serve to deter people from performing criminal acts. When we hear that there is a law against stealing, and that thieves are punished, this serves as a restraining factor in the melange of causes that lead to the acts we will perform.

Hobbes had his own view of what is involved in the matter of praise and blame. When we praise something, we are just registering our approval, and blame indicates that we disapprove. We approve and disapprove of many things when it is clear that no free will is involved. For example, we praise the pleasant weather and we condemn tornadoes, earthquakes and rabid dogs. No matter how much Bramhall kept protesting that the Hobbesian view would devastate our understanding of morality, Hobbes replied that his view was very compatible with morality and in fact, supported it. There is no conflict.

And so the controversy with Bramhall went on, for over 400 pages of not very cordial or polite objections to the other's views. Bramhall accused Hobbes of destroying the basis of religion and morality, and Hobbes kept saying that Bramhall did not understand the meanings of the terms that he was using. For Hobbes, arguments defending free will are really based on linguistic confusions and misunderstanding. Once the proper definitions are used, we can see that we have liberty, justice, morality and also necessity.

Hobbes' view has come to be called soft determinism or compatibilism, and has subsequently been defended by a number of distinguished philosophers. The same controversy that occurred between Hobbes and Bramhall can still be heard echoing around the corridors of contemporary philosophy. There are still philosophers who take the Hobbsian line that actually the free will-determinism conflict is only a pseudo-problem, the result of linguistic confusion. And still, there are others who say that no, there is a real problem and that if our actions are just the last dominoes in a long sequence of falling ones, then our concepts of morality and justice collapse as well. Four hundred years later, and the same controversy and the same arguments are still going round and round.

Hobbes and Descartes

Hobbes had the good fortune to meet the important intellectuals of Europe during his life, and he engaged in lively debate and discussion with many of them. One of the leading thinkers was Rene Descartes, who was not only a brilliant mathematician (the inventor of analytic geometry) and physicist, but was also a leading philosopher, and his *Meditations* was recognized in his time, and in ours, as being a seminal work in philosophy. In this work Descartes defended a dualist theory, a theory that claimed that human beings are composed of two substances, mind and body. The body, according to Descartes is basically a mechanical type of device, that obeys the laws the physics, but the mind is something quite different. It is not physical at all--it has no shape, no extension, and is made of no matter. Yet, it interacts with the body, and causes the body to move. The body also affects the mind, for when light strikes the eye and affects the optic nerve (Descartes was also an expert on the physiology of vision), the final step in the process is the production of an image in the non-physical mind. Among other things, Descartes set out his dualistic theory in his little book, *Meditations*, and Hobbes was asked to write some critical observations of it.

Hobbes, the rigorous materialist, was certainly unsympathetic to Descartes' view and he presented several criticisms of it. Descartes responded to these criticisms, and this provides us with a rare opportunity to see two of the founders of modern philosophy directly speaking to each other, debating issues which are still at the core of contemporary philosophy.

Descartes' *Meditations* consisted of six short chapters that in many ways set the agenda for the next four hundred years of European philosophy, especially in the fields of metaphysics and epistemology, the philosophical subjects that study what is real, and how we find out about it. In the first chapter Descartes presented what he considered a very strong argument for skepticism, the view that we cannot find out about anything. On his view we only know something if we cannot doubt it for any reason. Once he established this criterion for knowledge, he proceeded to raise all kinds of reasons for doubting everything that we think that we might know. He said that we should not rely on our senses because they sometimes deceive us. Even worse, we can not even tell if we are awake or dreaming. And even worse than that is that we cannot know even basic arithmetic truths like 2+2=4. Descartes doubted these basic truths on the possibility that there might be an evil demon that has nothing better to do than to spend all of his time deceiving us in ways we cannot even imagine. He gets us to believe that 2+2=4, and then laughs maliciously at us for being taken in by this falsehood. Descartes did not claim that there was such a demon; he only said that he doubted arithmetic because he could not rule out the possibility of there being a demon of this evil kind.

Descartes thought that his presentation of skepticism was the most powerful skeptical argument ever devised by any human. If he could show that even this argument did not rule out all knowledge, then once and for all, skepticism would be vanquished. In the last five chapters of the *Meditations* Descartes provided his answer to the skeptical arguments he raised in the first chapter. Hobbes was also very interested in skepticism and deception, although he was more concerned with the deception that occurs through the maneuvers of other people and not so much with the problems of our senses or with tricks of evil demons. But Hobbes had very little to say about Descartes' skeptical doubts. All Hobbes did was crab a bit that there is nothing new in wondering about whether we are awake or dreaming, as he said that this question was raised by Plato centuries ago. That is true enough, although even Plato did not suggest anything like an evil demon. Nevertheless, Hobbes was clearly not that interested in this part of Descartes' view.

What did incite Hobbes' critical inclinations was Descartes' famous argument in the Second Meditation in which he tried to show that even with all of the skeptical possibilities that he raised in the first chapter, there are still some beliefs that he cannot doubt for those very reasons. The first of these beliefs is that he exists. That cannot be doubted for any of the reasons he had stated previously. Even if his senses were deceiving him, or even if he was dreaming, or even if there was an evil demon controlling his mind and putting all sorts of beliefs into it, he still could not doubt that he existed. For supposing that any of these possibilities are true, they would not provide a reason for doubting his existence. Only one who exists can have senses that are deceptive, etc.

Hobbes would have been willing to accept this point of Descartes' but it was the next supposedly indubitable belief that raised the hackles of the materialist Hobbes. The next belief that Descartes said that he is certain of was that he is a thing that thinks. Descartes said that he cannot doubt that he is a being that has all kinds of mental activities, and furthermore that means that we can be certain that we have nonphysical minds where these mental activities take place. At this point Hobbes said, "Whoa".

Hobbes was willing to admit that some of the points that Descartes made, but not the final one. In Hobbes' view the fact that there is thinking does show that we exist, for there does have to be something that is doing the thinking. But this is no different than any other activity. From the fact that there is walking, we could just as well conclude that there must be a walker. What is questionable to Hobbes is the inference that Descartes made from the fact of thinking to the claim that whatever is thinking must be nonphysical.

Both Hobbes and Descartes agreed that there is a distinction between an activity and the thing that performs the activity. They also agree on the term to refer to this thing--they both call it "substance." But Hobbes claimed that there is only one kind of substance, and that is material objects, and Descartes' view was that there is another kind of substance which is very different than matter. For Hobbes all activities of a person--walking, leaping, thinking, dreaming, willing, perceiving-- are just modifications and changes of the basic material substance of a person. But for Descartes the activities can be divided into two distinct kinds and that means that a person is a combination of two substances that somehow interact with each other.

Unfortunately, the disagreement between Descartes and Hobbes was just asserted in Hobbes' objections and Descartes' replies. Hobbes did not provide any clear reasons why he insisted that all human activities must be attributed to only one substance. Descartes was quite dismissive of Hobbes' arguments, and said that he showed clearly that there must be two substances in the sixth chapter of the *Meditations*, but he did not discuss the arguments he mentions there. Hobbes mentioned that Descartes' view is the product of some linguistic confusion, which he did not spell out, and Descartes said that Hobbes' view of language is itself confused, but he also did not provide many details. At best, this was just a statement of positions, and no real argument was developed; however, the question of whether there is one substance or two, has been one of the perennial problems of philosophy ever since.

Another issue that was raised was whether the origin of everything we know about the world derives ultimately from our senses organs, or whether we have some other source for our beliefs, namely our reason. Once again, Hobbes took the parsimonious view--there is only one origin, the senses. This view came to be known as empiricism. Descartes, once again, had a dualistic view that came to be known as rationalism. We have two sources for our beliefs--our senses and also our reason.

Descartes set out his argument for rationalism in a famous discussion of a piece of wax. Descartes asked us to consider a piece of wax and to think of how we know of its qualities. We know the color, shape, texture, etc. of the wax by means of our senses, and Descartes was very careful to show that each one of our five senses provides us with some information about the wax. But then he asked us to notice what happens when we put the wax near a flame and melt it. Now each one of our senses tells us something different. Where once the wax was solid, it is now liquid. Where once it had a particular smell, now the smell has vanished. And yet, Descartes says, we think it is the same wax as before. This idea that it is the same wax must not come from our senses, because the information provided by every sense is that it has become something different. We have the idea that underlying the characteristics that have changed, something has remained the same. But where do we get this idea from if it does not come from our senses?

Perhaps, Descartes suggested, we get this idea of what the wax is from our imagination. For Descartes, the imagination is a faculty that provides us with distinct images of objects. But when we examine our idea of the wax, we find out that we think it is something that is flexible, extendable and moveable. To just consider the term 'flexible', we see that it means that we think the wax can take an infinite number of different shapes. But this is something that we cannot imagine, because we could never see an infinite number of different shapes in our mind's eye. Therefore, the origin of this idea about the wax does not come from our imagination, and the same thing would hold for the ideas of the wax being extendable and moveable. The source of these ideas must be something besides what we get from our sense experience.

This argument of Descartes' presented the basic viewpoint of Rationalism--the origin of *all* of our ideas about the world is not our senses. We have certain concepts, according to Descartes, that we do not simply derive from our experience. This point is one that Hobbes strongly disagreed with, and his objection was based on his views concerning language. The conflict between Hobbes and Descartes on this crucial matter was expressed by both of them in very cryptic terms, but what Hobbes seemed to be saying was that there are no ideas that we have about the wax that have an origin besides our senses. The reason is that given the way language works, we would have no way to name these so-called ideas. For the process of language involves providing names for particular things that we group together, and the only way we become aware of particular things is through our senses, and our senses only register what affects them in some kind of physical way. All of the ideas we have originate in motions that occur in the physical world.

In the objections and replies between Hobbes and Descartes, there is the interesting feature of seeing two thinkers who lived in the same time, and shared many basic assumptions, but are still talking at such cross-purposes that they fail to make any point of contact. Hobbes was assuming that materialism is true, and so he just dismissed Descartes' arguments that the mind is a different kind of substance. For Hobbes everything must begin with the movement of physical particles. For Descartes the activities of the mind cannot take place in a physical substance. Each one thought that the other's basic point was not really worth discussing. So the clash of titans is actually disappointing--two giants who while running toward each other miss each other completely, and unconcerned, keep going in their set directions.

Hobbes' Materialism

While Hobbes' controversy with Descartes does not provide us with many interesting arguments to consider, it does raise a final, and perhaps the most fundamental, issue involving Hobbes' ideas. Why was he such a staunch materialist? Materialism was certainly behind his belief in determinism, and it was probably the underlying basis for his atheism, if indeed that is what he was. Materialism also played a very important role in the development of his view of human nature and the subsequent ideas about the causes of war and the factors that can lead to peace. Materialism was clearly one of his fundamental beliefs, but what led him to it? Was it just an assumption on his part, or was it based on more basic beliefs and reasons?

Interestingly enough, while materialism was clearly a very important, and perhaps the most important underlying view of Hobbes' whole philosophy, he never provided a clear and definitive account of why he believed that materialism was correct. There are simply indications and brief remarks that can be used to reconstruct his underlying reasoning for materialism. We can wonder why Hobbes never made an explicit account of this matter. Was it perhaps his worry that materialism would be seen as actually disguised atheism? Hobbes always had this concern, and for good reason, but it cannot be used to explain why he never said, "This is why I am a materialist." After all, he was not shy about proclaiming to be materialist, and it was this conviction and not the explanation for it that would get him into trouble. So, it remains puzzling why there is no developed argument on the subject. Nevertheless, there are three inter-related considerations that can be retrieved from what Hobbes did say that seem to be the bases of his belief in materialism.

1) The Conceptual Aspect--The Structure of Language

Hobbes had the view that language consists of names that can be combined into propositions. When we use language, we are constantly making combinations, and it is very easy to fall into a trap of putting names together in one proposition that happen to conflict with each other. After all, names are just marks or signs, and one can write one down and then put another one down next to it and the result will certainly look like a proper proposition. The same is the case in our thought. We can think of one name and connect it with another name, and have the belief that we have made a coherent thought. But appearances can be very deceiving and we have to do some analysis to reveal that what we thought was an actual sensible proposition is actually confused and incoherent.

For example, one can write the proposition, 'The square is round', and that looks like English, but it just takes a moment's thought to reveal that this proposition has a serious problem. The name 'square' cannot be combined with the name 'round'. Each name stands for something that actually contradicts what the other name stands for. That is obvious. The proposition, 'That substance is incorporeal', is used by many philosophers and religious types, but according to

Hobbes, it is just as problematic as the 'The square is round.' This second proposition though requires some analysis to see the contradiction involved. The key term is 'substance'. 'Substance' is one of those names that should be examined carefully to see what it stands for. When we do this, it becomes evident, said Hobbes, that 'substance' is a term that has the name 'body' as one of its components, and 'body' is one of those very simple names that cannot be further analyzed. Thus, the proposition, 'That substance is incorporeal' amounts to the proposition 'That body is not a body' and that clearly is contradictory and incoherent. Thus, the claim that there are substances that are not material makes no sense.

There are many questions to raise, to be sure, about the above argument, and one of them is, why does substance have to be the name of something that is a body. Is this just an asserted claim on Hobbes' part, or is there some support for it? This leads to the second consideration--how we learn to name things.

2) The Acquisition of Language--Language and Sensation

Since Hobbes thought that language consisted of names, the problem of learning language is just a matter of explaining how we learn to provide names for objects. Hobbes said that all names are the result of a process that begins with sensations. Sensations of various kinds impinge on us, and start a chain of events that ultimately leads to the creation of an internal object, that Hobbes called a phantasm. For example, light reflects off a cow and hits my eye and affects my nerves and brain, and finally what results is an image, which is actually an object, although a very gossamer one, that exists inside of me. The light from a number of other cows strikes my eyes and causes similar images, and then I name these images 'cow', which is a matter of great convenience for memory and conversation.

This account of language is very fanciful on Hobbes' part, and it too raises many questions, but the point of main interest is that every name is the result of a sensation and every sensation is the result of being affected by some external material object. The term 'substance' is a name too, and so it can only name something that has some basis in sensation, and that means for Hobbes, 'substance' too is name of something that is a material object. The main point of this argument is that there would be no way to name something that is not material, and that is why the notion of an 'incorporeal substance' cannot make sense.

This account of language acquisition is certainly quite crude and it raises the following objection. Even if names are just the labels of sensations, as Hobbes claimed, why must all sensations have to be the result of a process that originates with material objects in the external world? Why can't we generate phantasms on our own? After all, we seem to do this in dreams. Why can't we create our own images, and then name them, and why couldn't one of these names be 'incorporeal substance?'

3) Motion

In answering the above questions, we arrive at what is the most basic point in Hobbes' views concerning materialism. Ultimately, for Hobbes, the answer lies in the nature of motion. He had certain views about motion that seemed to him to lead to the conclusion that materialism was true. A fundamental principle for Hobbes was that anything that moved must be moved by something else, or in other words, nothing can move itself. In holding this view, Hobbes was clearly influenced by his contemporary Galileo, who incorporated this principle into the new science of physics that he was developing.

The way Hobbes used the principle was to apply it to what occurs in our mental life. Our consciousness is a stream of moving thoughts. One idea or thought follows or leads to another--the stream constantly moves and is never still. These thoughts are the stream of phantasms, and for Hobbes, the phantasms themselves are physical objects, even if of a particularly airy kind. A particular phantasm is in the area where we pay attention to it, but then it quickly leaves, being replaced by some other phantasm. The process is not that different from one billiard ball hitting another. No billiard moves, on a level table, unless the cue or another billiard ball hits it. Similarly for Hobbes, no phantasm will move until it is moved by something else, and since the phantasms are themselves physical objects, they can only be moved by other physical objects. They cannot move themselves, since nothing can do that, and they cannot be moved by something non-material, because that cannot happen either. Given these basic principles of motion and Hobbes' view that phantasms are material, he thought there was no need to talk about anything incorporeal to explain what happens in the mind. We can explain everything that happens in the mental realm without having to refer to such strange things as incorporeal substances.

Thus, there is no non-material mind as Descartes argued for. There is no free will that Bramhall claimed. Human beings are just very complex material objects, and all of our actions and functions can be accounted for by principles that just refer to the actions of material bodies.

Assessment of the Three Considerations

These three considerations for materialism are loosely linked together, but clearly they do not constitute a serious argument for proving that materialism is true. There are simply too many problems and fallacies involved in them to think of them as comprising a weighty philosophical argument. Hobbes never really proved or demonstrated that there is no incorporeal substance; he just asserted that this idea is absurd. Also, he never showed that phantasms are themselves physical objects; he simply said that they are. It is not difficult to believe that Descartes was very unimpressed with Hobbes' views on these subjects, and that he reportedly said that the English philosopher would be wise to stick to political philosophy.

Was Descartes right? Since Hobbes seemed to just assume that materialism is true, and never really proved it, does it mean that this aspect of his philosophy should be dismissed? Perhaps there is another way to look at what Hobbes did that would make his writings on these issues more respectable. Hobbes did assume that materialism was true, as this was an axiom of his philosophy and not a theorem. But on the basis of this axiom, he tried to provide explanations for a number of psychological and ultimately also, political phenomena. Instead of worrying whether he offered any proof for his basic axiom, maybe it would be more useful and interesting to examine his explanations to see how successful they are. Philosophers have been flirting with a completely materialistic view of the world since ancient times, but before Hobbes, no one tried to spell out what such a view would actually look like. No one had tried to show how it would handle the kinds of phenomena that seem to be more compatible with saying that we have a non-physical mind. Hobbes was the first to try to give a mechanical-physical account of mental phenomena, and this attempt has continued and accelerated in our day. In providing this account and trying to push it as far as he did, he provided us with something that is of benefit in certain ways.

First of all, we can ask whether his materialistic view works. Does it help us to understand what is going on, but even more important to someone like Hobbes, does it help us predict and order our affairs? For all of Hobbes' metaphysical interests, he was very concerned about the practical matters of life, of how to live together in an orderly way and how to build a decent life together. His materialism can be seen in this light. If we assume it to be true, can we develop a psychological theory to explain human action that will be useful in avoiding war and promoting peace? Can we use materialism to perhaps develop a better understanding of medicine and how the brain works? Will this materialistic view be helpful in constructing a physics that will give us better control of our environment? If the assumption of materialism leads to richer, more fruitful, more useful theories in all these other areas, then perhaps it is an assumption that is well worth making.

However, even if materialism provides us with all of these benefits, there is still the question of whether it is true. For some reason, Hobbes never pursued this question directly. Nevertheless, what he did may still be helpful for those interested in this question. By setting out the main points of materialism in a clear way, Hobbes at least provided those who are interested in the truth of the theory with some important questions to examine. For example, if materialism is true, then some physical-material account has to be given for thoughts and sensations. Hobbes realized this very well, and he did give such an account. He provided a mechanical way in which a physical object can produce a "phantasm" in us, which can then lead us to moving in a certain direction. No doubt, Hobbes' account is crude and simple-minded, but any contemporary materialist is going to have to deal with the same issue. Just how do objects cause us to see things, and how do the images we see lead us to act? The process is enormously complicated, but Hobbes was still right. If materialism is true, somehow this process will have to be explained in material terms, whether it is in terms of complex molecules, electrical charges or whatever. If materialism is true, it has to deal with these phenomena in a satisfactory way. Hobbes knew that and provided the best account he could. The success of this whole attempt is still to be determined.

BIBLIOGRAPHY

Aubrey, James *Brief Lives* (London: Secker and Warburg, 1950)

Brown, Keith (editor) *Hobbes Studies* (Cambrdige, Massachusetts: Harvard University Press, 1965)

Descartes, Rene *The Philosophical Works of Descartes* translated by Elizabeth Haldane and G.R. T. Ross, volumes 1 and 2, (Cambridge, England: Cambridge University Press, 1967)

Gauthier, David *The Logic of the Leviathan* (Oxford: Clarendon Press, 1969)

Hobbes, Thomas *Leviathan* edited by Michael Oakeshott, (New York: Macmillan Company, 1962)

Hobbes, Thomas *Man and Citizen*, edited by Bernard Gert, (New York: Anchor Books, 1972)

Hobbes, Thomas *English works of Thomas Hobbes of Malmesbury*, edited by William Molesworth, volumes 1, 4 and 5 (London: John Bohn, 1966)

Kavka, Gregory *Hobbesian Moral and Political Theory* (Princeton: Princeton University Press, 1986)

Mintz, Samuel *The Hunting of Leviathan* (Cambridge: Cambridge University Press, 1969)

Missner, Marshall " Hobbes's Method in the Leviathan" in *The Journal of the History of Ideas* volume 38, number 4, 1977

Missner, Marshall "Skepticism and Hobbes's Political Philosophy" in *The Journal of the History of Ideas* volume 44, number 3, 1983

Popkin, Richard *The History of Skepticism from Erasmus to Descartes* (Assen, Netherlands: Van Gorcum, 1964)

Sorrell, Tom (editor) *Cambridge Companion to Hobbes* (New York: Cambridge University Press, 1996)

Thalos, Mariam "The Economy of Belief or, Explaining Cooperation Among the Prudent" in *American Philosophical Quarterly*, volume 35, number 4, October 1998.

Tuck Richard *Hobbes*, (New York: Oxford University Press, 1989)